FH

KEY
WOMEN
WRITERS
EDITOR: SUE ROE

IRIS MURDOCH

KEY
WOMEN
WRITERS
EDITOR: SUE ROE

IRIS MURDOCH

DEBORAH JOHNSON

Lecturer in English
University of Bristol

Indiana University Press
Bloomington and Indianapolis

Manufactured in Great Britain

Library of Congress Cataloging-in-Publication Data

Johnson, Deborah, 1950–
  Iris Murdoch.

  (Key women writers)
  Bibliography: p.
  1. Murdoch, Iris—Criticism and interpretation.
I. Title. II. Series.
PR6063.U7Z72 1987   823′.914   86–46238
ISBN 0-253-30104-1
ISBN 0-253-25454-X (pbk.)

1 2 3 4 5 91 90 89 88 87

For Deirdre, Amanda and Francesca

Titles in the Key Women Writers Series

Gillian Beer	*George Eliot*
Paula Bennett	*Emily Dickinson*
Penny Boumelha	*Charlotte Brontë*
Stevie Davies	*Emily Brontë*
Kate Fullbrook	*Katherine Mansfield*
Anne Green	*Madame de Lafayette*
Deborah Johnson	*Iris Murdoch*
Angela Leighton	*Elizabeth Barrett Browning*
Jane Marcus	*Rebecca West*
Rachel Blau DuPlessis	*H.D.*
Jean Radford	*Dorothy Richardson*
Lorna Sage	*Angela Carter*
Susan Sheridan	*Christina Stead*
Patsy Stoneman	*Elizabeth Gaskell*
Nicole Ward Jouve	*Colette*
Jane Heath	*Simone de Beauvoir*
Rebecca Ferguson	*Alice Walker*
Coral Ann Howells	*Jean Rhys*

Key Women Writers
Series Editor: Sue Roe

The *Key Women Writers* series has developed in a spirit of challenge, exploration and interrogation. Looking again at the work of women writers with established places in the mainstream of the literary tradition, the series asks, in what ways can such writers be regarded as feminist? Does their status as canonical writers ignore the notion that there are ways of writing and thinking which are specific to women? Or is it the case that such writers have integrated within their writing a feminist perspective which so subtly maintains its place that these are writers who have, hitherto, been largely misread?

In answering these questions, each volume in the series is attentive to aspects of composition such as style and voice, as well as to the ideas and issues to emerge out of women's writing practice. For while recent developments in literary and feminist theory have played a significant part in the creation of the series, feminist theory represents no specific methodology, but rather an opportunity to broaden our range of responses to the issues of history, psychology and gender which have always engaged women writers. A new and creative dynamics between a woman critic and her female subject has been made possible by recent developments in feminist theory, and the series seeks to reflect the

Iris Murdoch

important critical insights which have emerged out of this new, essentially feminist, style of engagement.

It is not always the case that literary theory can be directly transposed from its sources in other disciplines to the practice of reading writing by women. The series investigates the possibility that a distinction may need to be made between feminist politics and the literary criticism of women's writing which has not, up to now, been sufficiently emphasized. Feminist reading, as well as feminist writing, still needs to be constantly interpreted and re-interpreted. The complexity and range of choices implicit in this procedure are represented throughout the series. As works of criticism, all the volumes in the series represent wide-ranging and creative styles of discourse, seeking at all times to express the particular resonances and perspectives of individual women writers.

Sue Roe

Contents

Foreword

The experience of reading Iris Murdoch's novels as a process of intellectual and often emotional unsettlement has been aptly compared by Lorna Sage to 'the queasy excitement of a ride on a roller coaster'. Certainly it is hard for the critic to stand back from this experience and generalise about a writer whose whole literary and philosophical stance involves the most stringent testing out of generalisations. My aim in this short book has been to suggest a critical evaluation of the novels based on close reading and located within the context of contemporary feminist debate about the nature of 'women's writing'.

Such an approach, especially when conducted within the narrow limits of a very short book, will necessarily appear partial and *eccentric* (that is, at a tangent to the dominant cultural tradition in which Iris Murdoch writes). I undertook the work with some misgivings, being particularly anxious to avoid what might be construed as a 'narrowly feminist' reading. But the questions posed by the very nature of the project turned out to be more fruitful than I had at first supposed. I found myself directly engaged with some of the most problematical, puzzling and irritating aspects of the fiction, its often *explicit* assumption of 'masculinist' perspectives and values, and its curious reluctance, for the most part, to deal directly or non-ironically with women's experience. I have sought to read through and beyond the more obvious questions of sexual politics so as to understand some of the ways in which Iris Murdoch *does* explore and exploit her female creativity so as to question and even undermine the very assumptions which she appears to endorse.

Iris Murdoch's own stated views on feminism and on being a woman writer have changed remarkably little over the years. But they are interesting and thought-provoking and this may be the place to refer the reader to them. This is Iris Murdoch speaking in *Rencontres avec Iris Murdoch*, edited by Jean-Louis Chevalier, 1978 (p. 82), in an interview where she states her position with more than usual reflectiveness:

> About writing as a man, this is instinctive. I mean I think I identify more with my male characters than my female characters. I write through the consciousness of women in those stories which have different narrators, so I write as women also in those stories as well as men; but I suppose it's a kind of comment on the unliberated position of women.... I think I want to write about things on the whole where it doesn't matter whether you're male or female, in which case you'd better be male, because a male represents ordinary human beings, unfortunately as things stand at the moment, whereas a woman is always a woman! In fact of course I'm very interested in problems about the liberation of women, particularly, for instance, in so far as these concern education. I'm interested in them both as a citizen and as a writer, so they do come in to some extent.
> ... It's a freer world that you are in as a man than a woman. It's an interesting question and I don't think I've probably given the whole of the answer, but that's a part of the answer. A woman is much more self-conscious than a man, just as a black person is more self-conscious than a white person.

So the author does herself leave the door open for further speculation. But her continued stress on *education* as the crucial factor in determining the position of women and her rejection of the idea of any specifically female contribution which women may make to the 'human race' are certainly reflected in her explicit treatment of feminism in her fiction.

In the early novel, *The Sandcastle* (1954), the feminism of the schoolmaster hero, Mor, is convincingly linked to his decent, moderately socialist principles. It expresses itself first of all in a concern for his daughter's education and future career. His conventional, unimaginative wife, Nan, irritably rebuffs him, '"You think that reactionaries consider all women to be stupid, and so progressives must consider all women to be clever! I've got no time for that sort of sentimental feminism"' (pp. 12–13). It is characteristic of the author to frame her feminist statements in a cautious way, as she does all her political pronouncements. The association of feminism with educational issues is a vital part of the tradition of liberal humanism in which Iris Murdoch writes. Both as citizen and author she is sceptical about more radical positions. And while in another early novel, *The Flight From the Enchanter* (1955), she gave a sympathetic, vigorous and funny portrayal of the activities of a group of elderly suffragettes, in her two most recent novels, *The Philosopher's Pupil* (1983) and *The Good Apprentice* (1985), she caricatures those among her minor characters who are, in the phrase she uses, 'women's libbers', and the comedy works inevitably to undercut them. But this is to state the obvious, and I offer these observations simply as a point of departure.

In this short book it has not been my aim to relate Iris Murdoch's practice as a novelist to her stated views as an artist and to her philosophical imperatives. There is an impressive body of critical material which has explored these interconnections in a scholarly and leisurely way. The major full-length studies, by A. S. Byatt (1965), Elizabeth Dipple (1982) and Peter J. Conradi (1986; this last appearing just before the present study went to press) provide, with different emphases, detailed exposi- tions of the novels in the light of Iris Murdoch's complex yet lucid philosophical writings. I have been particularly concerned not to revisit familiar territory, especially in such a brief study where I have had to attend to a number of as yet unexplored questions. Where I do examine the relation between the novels and the philosophy I have been more concerned to stress some gaps and discontinuities than to suggest an overview.

In my particular task I have inevitably touched upon many different and still largely unexplored topics, such as Iris Murdoch's relationship both to modernist writing and to 'female Gothic', her reading and understanding of Freud, and her very individual handling of love and sexuality. In many such instances I have been able merely to indicate the areas of interest; the size and scope of this study as well as the limitations of my knowledge have not permitted a more thorough-going enquiry. I touch upon the issues of class and money only obliquely and very intermittently. Peter J. Conradi deals with these issues very intelligently and in some detail, from a non-feminist perspective (Conradi, 1986). These are some of the issues which I hope that future feminist studies of Murdoch will address. In general, I have opted for a questioning and open-ended approach ,rather than an exhaustive enquiry into specific topics. There is pleasure, too, in this second kind of activity, but it is of a different kind.

A small final point: I have chosen, with some hesitation, to refer to the author throughout as 'Iris

Murdoch' rather than, more fashionably and imper-
sonally, as 'Murdoch', which acknowledges the author as
unquestionably major but not as specifically female. But
I hope that the reader will bear in mind that I take 'Iris
Murdoch' to include 'Murdoch'.

I would like to thank my friends and colleagues at the
University of Bristol for their interest and support;
especially Rowena Fowler who provided many illuminating suggestions and comments in the early stages of
this book, and Myra Stokes who read the typescript.
Zenobia Venner offered me some valuable insights in
the course of our discussions. I would also like to thank
Jan Tarling for her time and her care in preparing the
typescript. My family has been involved all along,
especially my youngest sister, Francesca Johnson, whose
discernment proved invaluable when it came to cutting
and correcting the final draft. I wish also to record here a
particular debt of thanks to Sue Roe, whose warm
interest and involvement in this project extended far
beyond the call of her editorial duties. Finally, I would
like to thank Iris Murdoch for a memorable meeting in
which she was characteristically generous in answering
my questions and in offering her help. Although I do not
expect that she will entirely approve of the theoretical
basis of this study I would like to think that she may find
the questions raised interesting.

Acknowledgements

The author and publisher would like to thank the
following for permission to reproduce copyright
material: Iris Murdoch, Chatto & Windus Ltd and Viking
Penguin, Inc. for quotations from the novels of Iris
Murdoch.

A Note on the Texts

Page references for quotations from Iris Murdoch's novels are to the Triad/Panther editions, with the exception of the following:

The Italian Girl (Penguin, Harmondsworth, 1967)
A Fairly Honourable Defeat (Penguin, Harmondsworth, 1972)
The Black Prince (Penguin, Harmondsworth, 1975)
The Sacred and Profane Love Machine (Penguin, Harmondsworth, 1976)
Nuns and Soldiers (Penguin, Harmondsworth, 1981)
The Philosopher's Pupil (Penguin, Harmondsworth, 1984)
The Good Apprentice (Chatto & Windus, London, 1985)

Chapter One

Introduction: Questing Heroes

Iris Murdoch's novels pose in new and tantalising ways
the question of what it means to write as a woman, to
read as a woman. They disconcert and fascinate both
female and male readers by continually questioning
gender identity and transgressing gender boundaries.
At the same time they have notably not attracted the
attention of feminist critics. I am concerned to ask in this
study why this is so and to suggest how and to what
extent a reading of these texts may be modified and
enriched by a feminist critical perspective. I shall be
experimenting with various theories of sexual difference, various possible answers to the question of what
constitutes the 'feminine' in writing.

In the most obvious sense of the phrase Iris Murdoch
does not 'write as a woman'. Unlike so many of her
sister-novelists, Doris Lessing and Margaret Drabble
for example, she has not apparently been concerned to
explore what Elaine Showalter has called the 'wild zone'
of female experience, that area where women's experi-

1

ence does not overlap with men's.[1] On the contrary the
fictionalised masculine perspective is everywhere apparent in her novels. She is a female writer who likes
wearing male masks. In the seven novels where she em-
ploys a dramatised narrator from her earliest novel,
Under the Net (1954) to her latest but one, *The Philosopher's
Pupil* (1983), that narrator is invariably male. These
seven novels, which also include *A Severed Head* (1961),
The Italian Girl (1964), *The Black Prince* (1973), *A Word Child*
(1975) and *The Sea, The Sea* (1978), cover the thirty-odd
years' span of Iris Murdoch's career to date; they constitute, it will readily be agreed, some of her most distinctive and thoughtful work.[2]

The phenomenon of Iris Murdoch's male narrators is
one which I wish to explore at the outset. Elizabeth
Dipple in her important and illuminating study of the
novels, *Iris Murdoch: Work for the Spirit* (1982), bears, I
think, unwitting testimony to the powerful interest of
this phenomenon in the few sentences where she
touches upon it:

> One more technical issue is worth brief mention: the
> frequent presence of a male first-person narrator, and the
> absence of a corresponding female voice. . . . It is
> unprofitable to conjecture *why* Murdoch does it (because all
> the first-person narration takes place through corrupted
> male psyches, is this a veiled indication that men are more
> likely to be debased than women?), especially since she has
> said she is more comfortable there, and that seems to be
> that, since this study does not aspire to a psychoanalysis of
> the author.[3]

The writing here betrays the critic's deep interest in the
topic which she proclaims is so peripheral. The topic is
clearly not a 'safe' one; the text silently questions the
sense of the term 'comfortable' (whose comfort is

involved here?). In fact, a study of Iris Murdoch's narrators should not involve a psychological study of the author. What is in question here is a rhetorical strategy; her novels pose their own questions and do not need to be explained with reference to some supposedly more authoritative text.

Elizabeth Dipple does, however, go on to make an explicitly helpful comment about the phenomenon of male narration; it is 'something that should not work and does' and thereby she admits that the question of sexual difference does matter. I hope to show in the course of this chapter why Iris Murdoch's use of the male narrator works as well as it does.

Her curious preference for the male narrator is, I think, interestingly illumined by a passage from her philosophical work *The Sovereignty of Good*, in one of those apparently random connections between the non-fiction and the fiction which help to draw attention to the more puzzling elements in the fiction. In *The Sovereignty of Good* Iris Murdoch implicitly links the subjection to illusion, fantasy, the state of entrapment in the dreaming ego (which Plato calls *eikasia* and symbolises in the flickering, shadowy firelight of the Cave), with the gift of articulateness, the ability to manipulate language in order to have power over other people, and with the aesthetic fascination that language holds, the glamour of words. Inevitably her attitude to language partakes of her attitude to art in general; if art can all too easily degenerate into false patterns, lying consolations, then this must be true of language. *Goodness* (the generously disinterested awareness of the world outside the self) then becomes linked with silence and, even more revealing, with femaleness: 'Goodness appears to be both rare and hard to picture. It is perhaps most convincingly met with in simple people—inarticulate,

3

unselfish mothers of large families—but these cases are also the least illuminating'.[4] Of course this statement, from a feminist political perspective, makes a number of problematical assumptions. Why should these cases be the least illuminating? Does this statement simply reflect the middle-class intellectual assumption that there is only one culture and that 'inarticulate mothers of large families' don't have access to it and are therefore not 'interesting' from a philosophical point of view? Are the self-sacrifices and apparent silence of such women rather too readily approved of as 'goodness', a necessary underpinning of an all-too-corruptible social fabric? But it is misleading to isolate this single statement from its context in Iris Murdoch's work in general. Her writings elsewhere explore (implicitly and explicitly) what this statement seems to take for granted.

In her fictional versions of 'the pilgrimage from appearance to reality (the subject of every good play and novel)',[5] Iris Murdoch chooses as protagonist the figure most directly opposed to the simple inarticulate mother of a large family—that is, the childless male professional who is indeed articulate to the point of volubility—who has power and, in the full sense of the word, glamour (a glamour which Iris Murdoch illustrates, not always convincingly, by the sexual spell he wields over the various women who surround him). He is always in love with words and is often concerned with language as an instrument of power. He is usually artistically or intellectually highly gifted; he may be a theatre director (Charles Arrowby in *The Sea, The Sea*), a novelist (Jake Donaghue in *Under the Net* and Bradley Pearson in *The Black Prince*), or a well-known philosopher (Rozanov, the central power-wielder though notably not the narrator in *The Philosopher's Pupil*). However his gifts are always in some measure frustrated: Charles Arrowby finds that power over others involves guilt and so attempts to escape from his theatrical past, Jake Donaghue and Bradley Pearson are for different reasons 'blocked' and John Robert Rozanov has come, it seems, to the limits of philosophy; he is now 'tired of his mind'. Martin Lynch-Gibbon (*A Severed Head*) and Hilary Burde (*A Word Child*) are highly cultivated men who are, again for different reasons, scholars *manqués*. They have failed to pursue their true enthusiasms (history, languages), taking up instead jobs which palely reflect and even parody their creative and/or intellectual needs. All these characters are impelled by their sense of failure to some degree of deeper self-examination and an attempt to break some of the false patterns which have so far dominated their lives.

The status of the quester is from the start very much open to question and, more challengingly, so is the nature of his quest. All Iris Murdoch's word-children are unreliable narrators, flawed reflectors of the fictional worlds they inhabit. Patrick Parrinder, writing of the novels of B.S. Johnson, has this very apposite comment to make about the quest *topos* in modern English fiction:

> The more strictly religious the writer's temperament the more wary he is likely to be of the inauthentic, external fictions that surround him. At the heart of English Puritan culture is *The Pilgrim's Progress* with its image of the quest for righteousness as a constant and perilous confrontation with the phantoms and illusions met by the wayside. Only by exploding innumerable fictions does the steadfast pilgrim arrive at the truth.[6]

But there is always the possibility in Iris Murdoch's novels that the pilgrim's sense of his quest may turn out to be yet another illusion, another gratifying fiction. This is what happens to Hilary Burde in *A Word Child*. His original quest, in which he saw himself (as so many Murdochian heroes do) as a knight-errant, was the freeing of himself and his sister, Crystal, from the poverty and deprivation of their childhood through his ambitious and single-minded studies at Oxford: 'I was *busy*. Like a knight upon a quest I was dedicated, under orders. I had to rescue myself and Crystal, to get us out of the dark hole in which we had grown up and out into sunlight, into freedom' (p. 116). But he abandons his career after his affair with Anne Jopling and the driving accident through which he kills her together with her unborn child. In trying to redeem his past for the second time he ironically seizes upon another 'quest', this time a disastrous one, the entanglement with Gunnar's second wife, Kitty, who is seeking to arrange a reconciliation between Hilary and Gunnar, now twenty years after Anne's death. Hilary describes the second quest in ironically almost identical terms: 'I now had a task, I was like a knight with a quest. I needed my chastity now, I needed my aloneness; and it seemed to me with a quickening amazement that I had *kept* myself for just this time' (p. 200). This is a characteristic illusion of the Murdochian hero. For Hilary there never was a quest, apart from a T.S. Eliot-like return to the point of departure to 'know the place for the first time'.

Such fiction-making is portrayed by Iris Murdoch as a predominantly male activity. The women in her fictions are often given the role of undermining (comically or tragically) these sustaining fictions. Hilary, caught up in his Kitty/Gunnar quest and the obsession with his past, decides to 'cashier' (to use his own term) his fiancée, Tommy, so as to preserve his 'chastity' for the quest. In the final ironic twist of the plot it is Tommy who, jealous and disappointed, betrays Hilary to Gunnar and so unwittingly brings about the events which lead to

Kitty's death. Tommy is not to be so easily tidied away. In *The Black Prince* Bradley Pearson's quest, his 'ordeal', as he calls it, the confrontation with the Black Eros, is prematurely closed by the suicide of his sister, Priscilla. Her wrecked life has been revealed in brief and poignant glimpses while Bradley, Hamlet-like, has occupied the centre of the stage.

In her book on Sartre (*Sartre: Romantic Rationalist*) Iris Murdoch interestingly draws attention to the significant silences which occur in Sartre's novels due to his preoccupation with the existentialist quest and the isolated heroic questing consciousness:

> The lesson of *L'Etre et le Néant* would seem to be that personal relations are usually warfare, and at best represent a precarious equilibrium, buttressed as often as not by bad faith. We find nothing in the novels which openly contradicts this view. It is not only that the relationships portrayed in *Les Chemins* are all instances of hopelessly imperfect sympathies. . . . This in itself is nothing to complain of. Indeed it is in Sartre's ruthless portrayal of the failure of sympathy that we often most feel his penetration and his honesty. What does deserve comment is that Sartre acquiesces in the lack of sympathy in a way which suggests that his interest is elsewhere. He is looking *beyond* the relationship; what he values is not the possibility which this enfolds but something else. One feels this particularly perhaps in the treatment of Marcelle, who is dealt with hardly not only by Mathieu but by her author. Sartre is not really very interested in the predicament of Marcelle, except from the technical point of view of its effect upon Mathieu. Similarly we feel a touch of hardness in the portrayal of Boris's relations with Lola. We are not moved by Lola's situation—whereas we are pierced to the heart by the somewhat similar situation of Ellénore in *Adolphe*. And a part of the reason is that Lola's author does not care very much either; he *accepts* the position. It is not *here* that he has entered absorbingly into his work.[7]

Iris Murdoch sees these gaps in Sartre's work in general terms as a failure to give us 'a concrete realisation of what George Eliot called "an equivalent centre of self from which the shadows fall with a difference"'. But it is no accident that the spaces where she sees that Sartre 'has not entered absorbingly into his work', where 'he *accepts* the position', concern the portrayals of female characters. The heroic male consciousness in modernist fiction is particularly inclined to see the women it loves as objects in its mental landscape; their importance lies in the shape and direction which they give to the all-absorbing quest.

The male narration obviously de-centres the female point of view. As a woman writing, Iris Murdoch is clearly aware of what she is doing and can both seriously and playfully exaggerate this de-centring effect. Some of the reflections which she gives to her male narrators (as, notably, Charles Arrowby in *The Sea, The Sea*) are almost Jacobean in their intense misogyny, their habit of generalising about 'women'. In their arguments with the women who love them the narrators are forever drawing upon misogynist generalisation in order to score points (as Hilary does with Tommy in *A Word Child*). This is not to imply that Iris Murdoch's women don't generalise about 'men'; they sometimes do, but such generalisations are somewhat rare and impotent, set as they are in an age-old tradition of misogynist *sententiae* and the overall dominance of the male viewpoint in the novels. The male lover continually expresses his sense of superiority through his sheer powers of articulation, his marked tendency to cap and better or simply to interrupt the utterances of his 'mistress' (who is in any case usually younger and/or of inferior social status). Iris Murdoch is clearly preoccupied by the unequal power relationships which exist between men and women as she is by other kinds of unequal power relationship. Often she shows two inequalities reinforcing each other as they do in *A Word Child* when Hilary's crude sexual bullying of the beautiful and mysterious half-Indian girl, 'Biscuit', turns into an obliquely racist bullying: ' "What's your name, Miss Mukerji?" I did not expect her to tell me' (p. 55).

Iris Murdoch shows all human beings, men and women alike, as subject to *eikasia* and particularly to that form of *eikasia* which renders other people invisible. But it is much more likely to be a woman than a man who exclaims in exasperation, as Georgie does to Martin in *A Severed Head,* 'you've got to *see me*' (p. 105). Part of the reason why Iris Murdoch's male narrators fail to 'see' is precisely because they talk too much. Like Plato's bad art-object they cherish their volubility.[8]

This brief survey suggests that connections between the male hero, articulateness, power and the quest *topos* are presented with a considerable degree of deliberate irony on Iris Murdoch's part. Before exploring the novels any further I would like to raise some general questions about the device of male narration, questions to which we have been re-alerted by recent feminist criticism.

In terms of the current psychoanalytically-based theories of sexual difference, notably the work of Luce Irigaray, this 'male mimicry' can be seen as a potential means of undoing the repressive (patriarchal) structures encoded in language itself (Lacan's 'symbolic order'),[9] as a way of 'exposing through imitation'. As such it can point the way forward to a possible recovery of the operation of the 'feminine' in language. I shall briefly expound these ideas.

The thorny question of what *does* constitute the 'feminine' in writing has been well addressed by Mary

Jacobus in an essay which opens with an excellent brief introduction to some current theories of sexual difference.[10] She writes that

> Utopian attempts to define the specificity of woman's writing—desired or hypothetical, but rarely empirically observed—either founder on the rock of essentialism (the text as body), gesture towards an avant-garde practice which turns out not to be specific to women, or, like Hélène Cixous in 'The Laugh of the Medusa', do both. If anatomy is not destiny, still less can it be language.[11]

She then goes on to suggest a possible way forward:

> A politics of women's writing, then, if it is not to fall back on a biologically based theory of sexual difference, must address itself, as Luce Irigaray had done in 'Pouvoir du discours, subordination du féminin' to the position of mastery held not only by scientific discourse (Freudian theory, for instance), not only by philosophy, 'the discourse of discourses', but by the logic of discourse itself.

For Irigaray, notes Mary Jacobus, the systems of representation at work in discourse are 'masculine' in that they are self-reflexive and specular (woman is either ignored or seen as man's opposite) and so 'disappropriate women of their relation to themselves and to other women'. So the 'feminine' is that which is repressed or elided in discourse. A feminist politics in these terms 'would attempt to relocate sexual difference at the level of the text by undoing the repression of the "feminine" in all systems of representation for which the Other (woman) must be reduced to the economy of the Same (man)'.[12]

Luce Irigaray, notes Mary Jacobus, sees role-playing as central to the female subverting of male discourse:

Given the coherence of the systems at work in discourse, . . .
how is the work of language of which she speaks to be
undertaken at all? Her answer is 'mimetism', the role
historically assigned to women—that of reproduction, but
deliberately assumed; an acting out or role playing within
the text which allows the woman writer the better to know
and hence to expose what it is she mimics.

and she goes on to quote from Irigaray's 'Pouvoir du
discours':

To play with mimesis, is, therefore, for a woman, to
attempt to recover the place of her exploitation by
discourse, without letting herself be simply reduced to it. It
is to resubmit herself . . . to 'ideas', notably about her,
elaborated in/by a masculine logic, but in order to make
'visible', by an effect of playful repetition, what should have
remained hidden: the recovery of a possible operation of the
feminine in language. It is also to 'unveil' the fact that, if
women mime so well, they do not simply reabsorb
themselves in this function. *They also remain elsewhere.*[13]

Such playfulness is, Mary Jacobus stresses, political in
effect; the quest for specificity, for an elusive *écriture
féminine*, takes its impetus from the political and social
realities of women's experience: 'To postulate, as
Irigaray does, a "work of language" which undoes the
repression of the feminine constitutes in itself an attack
on the dominant ideology, the very means by which we
know what we know and think what we think'. The very
term 'women's writing' serves 'to remind us of the social
conditions under which women wrote and still write—to
remind us that the conditions of their (re)production
are . . . the sexual and material organisations of society,
which rather than biology, form the crucial determin-
ants of women's writing'.[14]

These theoretical insights certainly suggest ways of exploring theatrically and role-playing in Iris Murdoch's novels: they also help illumine the significant gap which separates the fiction from the philosophy, given Iris Murdoch's own insistence on the difference between philosophy and fiction as modes of discourse, and the distinctive nature of her practice within each mode. Although I shall not attempt to re-cast Iris Murdoch as an exponent of *écriture féminine*, I want to examine how far role-playing and male narration in her novels can be read as liberating devices, subversive of male-dominated structures and modes of perception.

An entirely opposite view of 'male impersonation' has been put forward by the more traditional literary-historical approaches implied in what has largely been Anglo-American feminist criticism. (The convenient distinction between French and Anglo-American feminist criticism is becoming increasingly out of date.) This criticism sees males impersonation as a form of evasion, an ultimately false bid for the universality, the neutrality historically carried by the male voice, a bid which literary and socio-economic history has made to a large degree necessary (an obvious instance being the adoption by early nineteenth-century female novelists of the male pseudonym). So Annis V. Pratt writes:

> Many woman novelists have even succeeded in hiding the covert or implicit feminism in their books from themselves. ... As a result we get explicit cultural norms superimposed upon an authentic creative mind in the form of all kinds of feints, ploys, masks and disguises embedded in the plot structure and characterization.[15]

Male impersonation in this view becomes an outstanding example of such feints, ploys, masks and disguises. And Sandra Gilbert and Susan Gubar discuss at length 'the aesthetic tensions and moral contradictions that threaten the woman writer who tries to transcend her own female anxiety of authorship by pretending she is male'.[16] However, while Charlotte Brontë's *The Professor* does seem to exemplify Gilbert and Gubar's theory, it might be argued that Emily Brontë's *ironic* use of male narration, Lockwood in *Wuthering Heights*, as one of several 'voices' in the narrative, is a much more flamboyant subversion of 'explicit cultural norms', and may be closer to what Iris Murdoch is doing with her male narrators.

How far, then, is Iris Murdoch's use of male narration a form of evasion, and how far is it a way of subverting the patriarchal structures and assumptions reflected in the texts? The problem is complex because so much more is involved in Iris Murdoch's use of male perspectives than mere ironic distance and implied didactic attitudes. There are various reason why these perspectives compel a sympathetic reading.

The reasons in general terms are bound up with the relationship between narrative and desire, with what Roland Barthes has described as the Oedipal trajectory of all narrative, the drive towards origins and ends, the quest for knowledge:

> The pleasure of the text is ... an Oedipal pleasure (to denude, to know, to learn the origin and the end), if it is true that every narrative (every unveiling of the truth) is a staging of the (absent, hidden, or hypostatized) father— which would explain the solidity of narrative forms, of family structures, and of prohibitions of nudity.[17]

The feminist semiotician, Teresa de Lauretis, in her book *Alice doesn't* (1984) has analysed the ways in which the discourse of Barthes (and of some other male structuralists) is ideologically loaded, or historically determined, so that the hero of narrative has to be seen as *male*, in obedience to a fundamental structuralist distinction predicated on sexual difference—the distinction between male-hero-human on the side of the subject, and female–obstacle-boundary-space, on the other.[18] Nevertheless, she writes sympathetically of the male Oedipal quest as it has been enacted throughout Western literature:

> It was not an accident of cultural history that Freud, an avid reader of literature, chose the hero of Sophocles' drama as the emblem of Everyman's passage into adult life, his advent to culture and history. All narrative in its movement forward towards resolution and backward to an initial moment, a paradise lost, is overlaid with what has been called an Oedipal logic—the inner necessity or drive of the drama—its "sense of an ending" inseparable from the memory of loss and the recapturing of time. Proust's title, *A la Recherche du temps, perdu,* epitomizes the very movement of narrative: the unfolding of the Oedipal drama as action at once backward and forward, its quest for (self) knowledge through the realization of loss, to the making good of Oedipus' sight and restoration of vision. Or rather, its sublation into the higher order attained by Oedipus at Colonus, the superior being capable of bridging the visible and invisible worlds.[19]

This description fits many of Iris Murdoch's novels well enough. In general terms, these trace the journey of a male hero into a comic version of Thebes, where he either remains caught for good in the toils of erotic (self) deception (Edmund in *The Italian Girl* and, arguably, Martin in *A Severed Head*) or he manages to survive the process and move towards a modest version of Colonus—'the world transfigured, found' as Bradley puts it at the end of *The Black Prince* (p. 391)—into a state not bound by his normal, narrow ego-consciousness. His vision is enlarged through the destruction of some of his most cherished illusions.

Iris Murdoch's love-plots accordingly often work as a series of unveilings, of the discovery of erotic substitutions. Charles's often repeated question in *The Sea, The Sea*, 'Who is one's first love?' finds its echo throughout Murdoch's fiction. Peter J. Conradi has drawn attention to the repetition of Oedipal family situations: sibling rivalry in *Under the Net, The Flight from the Enchanter, A Severed Head, Bruno's Dream, A Fairly Honourable Defeat, An Accidental Man, The Time of the Angels*; mother–daughter rivalry in *An Unofficial Rose, The Black Prince*; father–daughter incest in *The Time of the Angels*; brother–sister incest in *A Severed Head, The Bell* and *The Red and the Green*.[20] And it may be added that where incest does not appear literally in the plot it can figure metaphorically. In *The Good Apprentice* (1985), for instance, Edward's quest for deliverance from his despair leads him to find his natural father (the father 'absent, hidden, or hypostatized' in Barthes' terms) who appears as a most ambiguous love-object:

> Of course Jesse was his father. But he was, as if now filled up to the brim, so much more: a master, a precious king, a divine lover, a strange mysterious infinitely beloved object, the prize of a religious search, a jewel in a cave.   (p. 296)

Conradi, at one point in his book, discusses the novels in psychotherapeutic terms as an expression of 'the movement towards the saving of Eros, the clarification of passion or education of desire'.[21] He writes, 'Both growing up and paying attention for Murdoch are matters of struggling to perceive the world with less preconception, and to understand the provisionality of

15

life-myths which lead us to repeat roles in emotional systems whose patterns are laid down early'.[22] In this sense the male questing hero is Everyman and following his progress involves a certain degree of libidinal investment on the part of the reader as well as the author.

But what particular forms of identification are available here for *female* readers? We might experience, as de Lauretis argues in her analysis of quest narratives, a double or split identification, finding ourselves caught between 'the two mythical positions of hero (mythical subject) and boundary (spatially fixed object, personified obstacle)', a split analogous to that which 'cinema offers the female spectator: identification with the look of the camera, apprehended as temporal, active or in movement, and identification with the image on the screen, perceived as spatially static, fixed, in frame'.[23]

I want to argue that the playfulness of Iris Murdoch's quest-narratives works precisely to expose or foreground such a splitting of the female subject. There are various general ways in which this happens. The first is, as I have already argued, the tendency of the narrative to reveal the quest *topos* itself to be inadequate or illusory as a model or metaphor for living. The hero's search for psychological and spiritual healing runs into conflict with the other characters' readings of their own life-stories. The *female* Oedipus conflict (never a direct or sustained object of authorial focus) makes its presence felt as a complicating subtext; so, in *The Black Prince*, Julian's attachment to her father throws a questioning light on Bradley's exalted reading of his own love-story, and in *The Sandcastle* (1954), Rain's incomplete separation both as woman and as artist from her dead father is a shadowy and enigmatic area for Mor in his bittersweet romance with her. This relatively simple early novel, a seemingly straightforward love-story, is particularly interesting. Although Rain is seen primarily as *object*, her colourful clothes in particular emphasising her desirableness as female image, she is implicitly re-instated as female *subject* by the terms of her own Oedipal family romance. Her little scene with the ageing and despotic Demoyte (Chapter Seven, pp. 93–8) is characterised by a complicity with Demoyte, an innocent yet knowing acceptance of his wistful gallantry, and suggests that Rain adopts this *pattern* of behaviour towards older men in general. With a beautiful structural subtlety this scene directly follows the more famous scene (Chapter Six) where Rain and Mor drive together into the woods and accidently overturn Rain's beautiful and expensive Riley into the river. (The car is a source of nagging anxiety to Mor; Rain has put it out of her mind when we next see her.) The juxtaposition of the scenes comments upon the enigmatic areas in Rain's personality, areas which remain closed to Mor's limited knowledge and awareness.

A final point which needs to be made about Iris Murdoch's handling of Oedipal situations is that the Freudian tensions are characteristically diffused by comedy. This is the case throughout the playfully Freudian novel *A Severed Head*. A pointer to the Oedipal logic of Martin's progress is provided in the (comically explicit) dream which Martin has at the beginning of Chapter 21 (pp. 137–8). The dream is constructed with an almost mechanical lucidity so as to point to Martin's hidden castration complex. Martin dreams that he is skating with his sister, whose image the reader sees implicitly but unmistakably to resemble Honor Klein. The condensed figure of Martin's sister/Honor gives way to a second condensed figure who represents both Martin's father and Honor. This mildly terrifying image is another 'severed head' (the sword is recalled from Martin's witnessing of Honor's Samurai sword display):

> . . . he glided on towards me with increasing speed, his huge Jewish face growing like a great egg above the silken wings of his gown. I swung the sword in an arc before him but as it moved the blade came away and flew upwards into the winter darkness which had collected above us. Clinging in fear and guilt to what remained in my hand I recognized my father.
> (p. 138)

The Freudianism of the dream is rather tongue-in-cheek, illustrating the suave psychoanalyst Palmer's theories concerning the 'mechanical' nature of the psyche. At the same time, it points to the underlying family drama in which Martin is caught, and which he keeps re-enacting with erotic substitutions. From a feminist viewpoint it is interesting that the most important of these erotic substitutions, Honor, should embody the division which according to feminist semiotic theory splits the female subject. Honor is the object of Martin's quest. She is taboo-object, sister in the royal incestuous brother–sister pair, severed head, Medusa as site of the original castration trauma ('the female genitals feared, not desired' (p. 45)). To that extent she remains opaque, veiled, within the story. But Murdoch gives Medusa a voice. Honor is highly articulate and is well qualified to explain her status as taboo-object to Martin: she functions as subject too. The logic of the interconnected events in the plot suggests that Honor is rather better than Martin at getting what she wants and it hints at an alternative reading of the novel in which Honor herself might function as a more canny female version of the questing hero.

These various feminist theories suggest some ways of

articulating the complex relationship of the female author to her fictions. The question of how and to what extent Iris Murdoch inscribes her female presence into her text is, I think, central; it is related to what many critics and reviewers have seen as her 'comfortable' distance or detachment from her characters, her careful 'expunging of the self from the work of art' in A. S. Byatt's phrase, and consequent reluctance or inability to 'inhabit her action' as fully as she might.[24]

A closer look at the individual roles and masks presented through the dramatised male narrators (who, after all, differ very much among themselves) should reveal something of their function within these strangely elusive novels and begin to provide some answers to these questions.

Chapter Two

The Role of the Narrator

Under the Net (1954) (as the back of the Triad/Granada paperback edition reminds us) was hailed by a reviewer in *The Sunday Times* as 'a real achievement of entertainment and impersonation'. The word 'impersonation' is a clear pointer to what Iris Murdoch is doing in all these novels; she is creating *personae*, masks. Her first novel notably expresses her preoccupation with the theatre, with theatrical imagery, with the springs of cunningly contrived illusion. It emphasises masks and roles, which continually appear as symbols in the narrative. But the most important 'mask' in the novel is Jake himself, the male narrator whom the female author is impersonating.

Jake is the hero of a comedy which works to dissolve false *personae* and set assumptions, to show how our perceptions of gender differences, for instance, are codified in particular ways at particular times, and how we continually exploit and transgress these codes in our search for love and power. So character and action are presented as comically subordinate to setting and situation. When Jake encounters Anna in the 'props' room of her Mime Theatre, the richly chaotic theatrical bric-à-brac is described in a memorable passage which determines the entire course of the following scene:

> It was like a vast toy shop that had been hit by a bomb. In my first glance I noticed a French horn, a rocking-horse, a set of red-striped tin-trumpets, some Chinese silk robes, a couple of rifles, Paisley shawls, teddy bears, glass balls, tangles of necklaces and other jewellery, a convex mirror, a stuffed snake, countless toy animals, and a number of tin trunks out of which multi-coloured costumes trailed. Exquisite and expensive playthings lay enlaced with the gimcrack contents of Christmas crackers. I sat down on the nearest seat, which happened to be the back of the rocking-horse, and surveyed the scene. (p. 39)

In Jake's survey of the 'scene', Anna appears in this new element as an 'improbable' being, 'a very wise mermaid rising out of a motley coloured sea' (p. 40), and later, lying amid the multi-coloured debris after Jake has kissed her, a 'great doll', 'a fairy-tale princess tumbled from her throne' (p. 43). She appears as two-dimensional as the objects which surround her, and in this context action is likewise simplified; it too becomes theatrical or, rather, cinematic:

> I took her wrist, and for an instant saw her eyes wide with alarm, very close to mine, and then in a moment I had thrown her, very carefully, onto a pile of velvet costumes in the corner of the room. My knee sank into the velvet beside her, and straightaway a mass of scarves, laces, tin trumpets, woolly dogs, fancy hats and other objects came cascading down on top of us until we were half buried.
> (p. 40)

and, again, a little later:

> I took the wrist with the watch upon it, and twisted it until I heard her gasp. . . . I kept her pinioned, but released the tension enough for us to kiss. (pp. 42–3)

Jake's actions, like the setting, interestingly deflect any realistic impact that this erotic encounter might have had; it becomes deliberately illusionistic, recalling, as does so much else in the book, the conventions of Hollywood cinema, 'fifties-style.

Jake draws on such conventions in moments of indecision or fear or simple embarrassment. This is exactly what happens when he meets the formidable 'bookie', Sacred Sammy:

> I took a gulp of the whisky and put on my belt, endeavouring to wear the expression of one who, contrary to appearances, is master of the situation. The films provide one with useful conventions of this kind. I looked Sammy up and down with deliberation. (p. 71)

With Anna, Jake's cinematic strong-guy stance enables him to avoid the kind of encounter that seemed almost inevitable with a long-lost 'old flame', an encounter full of awkward silences and polite clipped exchanges: 'In a moment we should be talking soberly like two old acquaintances. I wasn't going to allow this' (p. 40). Jake breaks taboos, traversing roughly the distance that in polite intercourse separates one person from another. But it is, as he realizes, a somewhat precarious 'act', and it is comically undercut by Anna's sister, the intelligent film star, Sadie, whom Jake finds at the hairdresser's:

'You won't start being afraid of me, I suppose?' I said, leering at her in the glass. Sadie went off into peals of laughter. 'Jake, darling, no, you're just too utterly harmless!' she called out.

I didn't so much care for this turn in the conversation.

(p. 53)

The rose-tinted mirrors in the hairdressing salon, a beautifully apt image in a novel which so stresses the deceptiveness and charm of surfaces, have flattered Jake a little earlier in the narrative. Looking for Sadie he sees himself in them as quester, hero, 'like a prince in a fairy-tale' (p. 51), as he encounters one reflected pair of enquiring female eyes after another. The women reflected in the mirrors appear to him in a series of suggestive synecdoches: 'elegant heads . . . in various stages of assembly', 'a row of well-dressed backs', 'a large number of fascinated female eyes'. The whole narrative is pervaded by images of women as seen through Jake's eyes, women wearing masks of make-up, elaborate coiffures, high-heeled shoes. Jake is the detached male observer who seems to carry something of the author's own fascination with and detachment from the fashions and conventions which codified femininity in the early 'fifties, when the novel came out. But Jake's control of the perspective, as in the encounter with Sadie, is only apparent; the ironic presence of the female author makes itself felt behind the male *persona*. Jake *seems* very much in control when he describes Madge ('everyone's idea of a pretty girl'), the young typist in whose house he has been living:

Her real employment is to be herself, and to this she devotes a tremendous zeal and artistry. Her exertions are directed along the lines suggested to her by women's magazines and the cinema, and it is due simply to some

23

spring of native and incorruptible vitality in her that she has not succeeded in making herself quite featureless in spite of having made the prevailing conventions of seduction her constant study.   (p. 10)

Yet as the narrative proceeds the joke is surely on Jake, who is not immune to parallel charges and who at crucial moments gladly draws upon the available models of (male) seduction.

This is an elegant novel of surfaces which emphasises the extent to which we all play roles. Jake sees the difference between the sexes as largely a question of role-playing, women being 'always a little more un-balanced by the part they have to act' (p. 29). In the course of the novel Jake comes to appreciate something of the ungraspable fluid reality that underlies the changing conventions of social behaviour and artistic expression. Here Iris Murdoch's vision comes close to Sartre's but there is a significant gap, as A.S. Byatt has pointed out:

> Sartre's heroes agonize and contemplate in a lucidly tortured solitude. . . . There is a sense in which the comic and densely populated worlds of Iris Murdoch's first two fantasies are a kind of meaningful game with the Sartrean universe. Jake tries an internal monologue, but discovers that the world is full of other people whose views he has misinterpreted but *can learn*. . . . No single view of the world, no one vision, is shown to be adequate. . . . [1]

The wording of the last sentence suggests that Iris Murdoch may be closer here to Virginia Woolf than to Sartre. And indeed she shares something of Woolf's striving after an aesthetically rendered *plurality* of vision and her stress on human sympathy and interconnection, She also shares Woolf's playfulness, her subverting of set assumptions about gender roles and gender indentity through a dramatically presented series of roles and disguises (I am thinking particularly of Woolf's last novel, *Between the Acts* (1941)). And like Woolf's *To the Lighthouse* (1927) with its depiction of the philosopher, Mr Ramsay, who persistently sees himself as 'leader of a doomed expedition', *Under the Net* provides a good-humoured critique of the male questing hero of so much modernist (and post-modernist) fiction, of the almost solipsistic intensity which accompanies his sense of his quest. At the conclusion of the novel Jake has found his true quest, his 'path', but he does not celebrate it in a grand self-justifying gesture. He is last seen puzzling over the workings of genetics as he contemplates a mixed litter of newborn kittens.

The *masculinity* of Jake as dramatised narrator acts as a guarantor of such a truth-seeking *plurality* of vision in the book. We watch Jake in the process of continually revising and questioning his assumptions about maleness, femaleness, sexual glamour, personal and political power. The author's own femaleness is registered in this playful exposure of stereotyped models of human behaviour, and in the space which she carefully maintains between herself and her male narrator, a space which is beautifully conveyed through the persistent theatrical imagery of masks, roles, décors, stage properties, all of which influence the ways the characters behave towards one another.

The theatrical metaphor is present to a lesser degree in *A Severed Head* (1961), the next novel to employ a male narrator. As unfaithful husband and lover, Martin Lynch-Gibbon has been involved when the novel opens in a 'prolonged and successful masquerade' (p. 21). Unlike *Under the Net*, *A Severed Head* draws attention to the abyss which lurks behind apparently civilised behaviour.

Iris Murdoch

The masquerade is punctuated by moments of emotional and physical violence. (Martin is an amateur boxer, in contrast to Jake, who is a former amateur judo wrestler.) Martin's violence is unleashed at three crucial moments in the narrative, once against Georgie, once against Honor and finally against Palmer (the striking of Georgie and the attack on Honor are clearly displacements of the anger which Martin is initially incapable of expressing against Palmer). Whereas the small and versatile Jake has a brilliant ability to improvise, to wriggle out of tight corners (the attractive thing about him is that, a practical joker himself, he can enjoy his own discomfiture), Martin takes some hard knocks.

At the beginning of his narrative Martin appears confident and secure; his generalisations come faster than do Jake's: he resembles an urbane comedy-of-manners hero in his way of continually asserting opinions as facts: 'In almost every marriage there is a selfish and an unselfish partner. A pattern is set up and soon becomes inflexible, of one person always making the demands and one person always giving way' (p. 14). Martin addresses his audience as an audience of fellow-*men*; he invites its complicity; he implies that his listeners are involved in much the same series of deceptions and self-deceptions as he is: 'I had, of course, misled Georgie about the success of my marriage. What married man who keeps a mistress does not so mislead her?' (p. 14). Martin is obviously playing to the gallery. But the security of his stance is soon undermined by the series of unnerving disclosures which leads him eventually to his obsession with Honor Klein (an obsession which makes nonsense of all his previously-held notions about his own social and sexual being) and to the wittily improbable conclusion in which Honor decides to take

26

her chance with him. As Douglas Jefferson has pointed out: 'Probability has been distorted to produce a schematic, sardonically-conceived reversal of Martin's whole existence, and Honor is part of the design'.[2] Such contrivance does not rule out the audience's interest in Martin's psychological development, his brusque discomfitures, his shocked self-realisations. The strength of his rhetorical presence has ensured all along the interest (ready or reluctant) of his audience/readers. As *female* audience, excluded from the male audience that is implied within the fiction, we find ourselves admitted by a curious side-door as the ironies of Martin's position gradually become apparent. It is *only when* we close the novel and look back at it as a whole, that the outrageous degree of narrative contrivance, what I might call the whole Murdochian swindle, becomes evident; in the *process* of reading, one event follows the next with a certain emotional logic.

The often subtle ironies of *A Severed Head* do not stem simply from the time-honoured use of first-person narration to convey a limitation of awareness. A complex, specifically female perspective is at work and Iris Murdoch realises subtleties of effect which I suspect were unintended even in this apparently most contrived of novels. For example, Martin says of his love for Georgie: 'I loved her with a sort of gaiety and *insouciance* which was more spring-like than real spring, a miraculous April without its pangs of transformation and birth' (p. 20). And on the same page Martin goes on to refer to Georgie's pregnancy and abortion, 'the time of the child'. At the end of the previous chapter we were told that Georgie had become pregnant 'last spring' and that 'there was nothing to be done but to get rid of the child'. Georgie herself remains in an important respect unknown to Martin, as he admits: 'What vast wound that catastrophe had perhaps made in Georgie's proud and upright spirit I did not know' (p. 13). Here the writing works to dissolve the codes in which the experience of romantic love is inscribed in our culture (Martin's 'miraculous April'), thereby undoing a double repression, the repression of the bodily and the repression of the female.

Through the ironic juxtaposition and gaps in Martin's narrative the author makes her female presence felt. In this context there is an obvious irony in Martin's use of the word 'object', in a way which expresses his fundamental acquisitiveness. This is how he describes his wife, Antonia, early on in the novel:

> She has long goldenish hair—I prefer women with long hair—which she wears usually in an old-fashioned knot or bun, and indeed 'golden' is the best general epithet for her appearance. She is like some rich gilded object over which time has cast the moonlit pallor of a gentle veneer . . . (p. 16)

The epithets 'golden' and 'gilded' will later acquire disturbing connotations in the dangerous association of Antonia and Palmer as Martin finds himself excluded from relation and possession. At present they convey Martin's gratifying sense of possessing an erotically and aesthetically pleasing 'object' whose value in his highly possessive view of the marriage relationship can only be enhanced with time. Honor Klein, however, when he collects her at Liverpool Street Station (a favour rather ignominiously undertaken for Palmer) appears as an 'object' of a different kind. He defends himself against the brusqueness of her observations (' "This is an unexpected courtesy, Mr Lynch-Gibbon" ') with the thought, 'I don't care what this objects thinks of me' (p. 57). And the curving seam of Honor's thick knitted stocking which reminds him 'just for an instant that she was a woman' (p. 58) is an implicit ironic reminder of the occasion when Martin 'possessively' watches the charmingly bohemian Georgie draw on a pair of peacock blue stockings which he had given her (p. 8).

These and similar ironic echoes and reminders work against the apparent collusion of author and male narrator. The text mimics and thereby exposes some stock cultural assumptions about women and erotic experience as Martin is dispossessed of both Antonia and Georgie, and impelled towards the 'terrible object of fascination' which Honor has, as she points out, become for him (p. 184). And while the author powerfully communicates Martin's dazzling sense of risk and self-realisation she does, nevertheless, hint at perspectives other than Martin's (in the terrible fate of Georgie, for instance), and discreetly leaves it open to question as to whether Martin's passion will survive the transition into the ordinary, human, 'waking world' (p. 207).

The Italian Girl (1964) is the shortest and most obviously 'patterned' of Iris Murdoch's novels and as such constitutes an interesting Murdochian paradigm. While *A Severed Head* emphasises the theatricality involved in ordinary 'civilised' social behaviour, the 'masquerade', *The Italian Girl* presents a kind of Freudian dream-narrative in which, often without a moment's warning, the characters are transformed by the violence of their passions into metaphorical monsters. The novel has not, in general, received favourable critical attention. Elizabeth Dipple describes its problematic function as 'an unintentional parody of its author's usual amusement and expertise in plot turns'.[3] The tendency to self-parody is present in the detail of the writing, in the microcosmic workings of the style. The following snippet of dialogue between the narrator, Edmund, and

Isabel (who has lost her lover to her daughter, Flora) is fairly representative:

> 'You are raving,' I said. 'Otto could so easily find out, and—'
> 'I know. I feel like a ship moving steadily towards an iceberg. But I can no other. Don't you see I'm *in extremis*? The only question is, when Otto finds out, will he kill David or me or both.'
> (p. 110)

The descent from stilted archaism and learned tag into the banality of the last sentence is not offered as realistic, dramatically conceived speech, as character in action; what is in evidence is a certain pleasure in outrageous contrivance of plot and situation. Isabel's speech does not belong to any recognisable social register. (It's certainly hard to bear in mind here that she speaks with a Scottish accent.)

Much of the dialogue is like this. A serious problem does arise where it is used to handle poignant and complex moral issues, such as the very young Flora's unwanted pregnancy (' "You don't know what it's like, you men. . . . I have this thing inside me like a monster growing, growing" ' etc., p. 53). The Flora episode all too clearly has a function in the overall *scheme* of the novel (Isabel is left at the end of the story happily pregnant by the same man, and the Oedipal drama, it is hinted, will continue). In such episodes the degree of authorial contrivance and detachment seems excessive: it may be said that this novel, at any rate, doesn't value the experience it's made of.

At the heart of the problem here is the handling of the male narrator, Edmund. If Elizabeth Dipple is right in surmising that this is an early novella, resurrected and published out of sequence,[4] this would help account for the unsatisfactoriness and undeveloped nature of

Edmund as *persona*. It is never clear how far the author is in collusion with him. He lacks the rhetorical presence of Iris Murdoch's other dramatised narrators and has no clear relationship (of complicity or otherwise) with his readers. The writing reads as a reluctant confession rather than a spirited apologia (to compare the novel with its closest relative, *A Severed Head*). While the *plot* acts as an implicit critique of Edmund, the *tone* is wavering and uncertain, particularly in the scenes where Edmund confronts Isabel and Flora, as the following passage shows:

> It was always a trick of my nature to be subject to these sudden enchantments of the visible world, when a particular scene would become so radiant with form and reality as to snatch me out of myself and make me oblivious of all my purposes. Beauty is such self-forgetting. Yet in all this I saw Flora clearly, saw that her great-skirted dress was not white, as I had seen it before, but a very pale blue and covered with little black sprigs of flowers.　(pp. 47–8)

The pompous tone of the first half of this with its vague gesture towards 'all my purposes' is curiously repellent. Intentionally so? I wonder. It is hard to detect any saving humour, any ironical doubling of perspective. (The writing here can be contrasted with the comedy the later Murdoch extracts from Charles Arrowby's self-congratulating aesthetic perceptions in *The Sea, The Sea*, where the journal form provides the ideal narcissistic medium.) The second half of the passage, however, works well to convey the shift of perception by which Edmund sees Flora's dress clearly for the first time; it suggests a parallel moral focusing upon Flora as Edmund sees her step out of the pretty picture frame and confront him as a person who is damaged and angry. In the novel as a whole the details of Edmund's visual perceptions are vividly rendered (giving the whole narrative something of the heightened colouring and economy of a dream) while there is a curious absence at its centre, the hollowness of its narrator, which is ultimately the self-absenting of the female author.

But the female author cannot absent herself entirely. The complexities of her position are well conveyed by the central symbol in the novel, 'the dreaming, swimming dazed Eve of Gislebertus' at Autun Cathedral. This exquisite image exerts an almost hypnotic power on the writing but its significance is highly ambiguous. '"Ah, if I could have ever carved anything like that . . ." ' exclaims the sculptor, Otto, and yet he has just recalled the image in connection with his unhappy marriage to Isabel and what he sees as female evil. He tells Edmund:

> Sometimes I think women really are the source of all evil. They are such dreamers. Sin is a sort of unconsciousness, a not-knowing. Women are like that, like the bottle. Remember that dreaming Eve at Autun, that dreaming, swimming dazed Eve of Gislebertus? Ah, if I could have ever carved anything like that. . . .   (p. 4)

This glimpse of the dazed Eve recurs much later as Edmund, confronted by the emotional havoc Isabel seems unconscious of creating, recalls and corroborates Otto's words: 'I recalled what Otto had said about the dreaming Eve of Autun, the root of all evil. Isabel simply didn't seem to know what she was doing' (p. 110). Behind this is the pun of Milton's Adam, 'O Eve, in evil hour . . .'. But what is the attitude of the author here? How far is she corroborating the words of her narrator? The events of the narrative at this point certainly bear Edmund out, and with him the ancient misogynist wisdom which associates women with the flesh, and so with evil.

On the other hand there is a wider pattern of events which does not bear Edmund out. Edmund, initially seen as everyone's advisor, in Isabel's words 'a good man . . . a sort of doctor . . . the assessor, the judge, the inspector, the liberator' (p. 36) (a view of his powers which understandably alarms him), gradually and reluctantly becomes reinvolved in the Oedipal family drama. The narrative offers a psychologically most perceptive study of Edmund's voyeurism. It resembles a Freudian dream-narrative in its suppression of the logical connections between events (because . . . therefore), connections which have to be inferred from simple sequence (and . . . and).[5] So the crucial question, why does Edmund forget his breakfast-time appointment with Flora who has desperately sought his advice, finds an answer in the dreamlike sequence of events which has unfolded on the previous night (in the chapter called 'The Magic Brothel'). The uncanny encounter with Elsa whom Edmund takes at first to be Flora ('Flora despairing, Flora running mad'), the worms' dance, the discovery of Elsa's and Otto's summerhouse haunt, the seductive behaviour of Elsa and the 'voyeur-like complicity' with which her brother, 'the delinquent Levkin', speaks of her all have the effect finally of causing Edmund reluctantly and implicitly to confront his own sexuality, the instinctual side of his nature which he has been conveniently ignoring for so long. The 'instinctive disgust' and 'moral nausea' which he had felt, confronted with the fact of Flora's pregnancy, proves in the events of the narrative to be a signal of his awakened sexual interest in her and in women generally. Flora's name in any case suggests her ambiguous nature of goddess/harlot as seen through Edmund's eyes, and she has a double in the overtly sexual, half-crazed Elsa. Flora is implicitly associated with Eve (as are Elsa and

Isabel explicitly) and perhaps with Marvell's little T.C. as she moves from innocence into experience against a background of flowers and vegetation.

So while the sequence of events can bear Edmund out at the local and particular level, it shows up the limitations of his vision when taken as a whole. It is possible to see an implicit feminist perspective at work in the silent commentary provided by this larger narrative pattern. The misogynist viewpoints expressed by Otto and Edmund are in the end undermined as the men prove to be without authority to judge the women. The most authoritative figure in the story is the virtually invisible and long-exploited maid, the Italian girl, Maria Magistretti, and she judges no one, although for various reasons the others are all afraid of her judgement. Ostensibly the blame for the monstrous emotions which stalk the house is carried by Lydia, the terrible Devouring Mother who looms over the two brothers, the 'one that eats' and the 'one that watches'. But Lydia is dead and therefore *must* take the blame; she cannot defend herself. It is from the Italian girl herself that Edmund in the last pages of the novel looks forward to hearing Lydia's 'true epitaph'.

The implicit logic of events has the effect of deconstructing some conventional misogynist attitudes. It opens up a perspective in which the discrepancy between the real women and their larger-than-life projection in the imagination of the men is suddenly revealed. On the other hand, I would not want to argue that *The Italian Girl* deals with these questions particularly successfully. Its contradictions and ambiguities do not seem to me to be ultimately fruitful in artistic terms; they merely indicate a fascinating and unresolved authorial puzzlement over questions of writing and gender. The author does not know what to do with her male narrator, and the writing veers unsteadily between excessive collusion and excessive detachment.

The vagueness in the central *persona* corresponds to a curious vagueness in the geographical location and setting. The action takes place somewhere in 'the north'; there is a passing reference to 'collieries'. This 'north' functions as a perfunctory symbol for the primitive Gothic world in which the characters find themselves enclosed. Isabel, the character who is most conscious of her imprisonment, describes the 'north' as being 'Gothic', like her uncouth husband. The vagueness here may be contrasted with the splendidly precise evocation of London in *A Severed Head*, and of the detailed ways in which Martin's psychological and emotional development is registered in the different perceptions of 'London' which he conveys to his audience, the fog in Liverpool Street Station, the misty, fitfully illumined Thames, the 'damp dolphin-entwined lamp-posts' of the Victoria Embankment, the telephone box which seems to announce to Martin the nature of his terrible obsession. Here the narrator's vision is inseparable from his rhetoric. Compared with the other novels *The Italian Girl* lacks a body and a heart; it is a poetic curiosity, a 'severed head'.

By complete contrast, *The Black Prince*, published nine years later (1973), is a complex and brilliant exploration of the relationship between the author and her male narrator. This novel beautifully illustrates what Luce Irigaray understands by 'mimetism'—'an acting out or role playing within the text which allows the woman writer the better to know and hence to expose what it is she mimics'.[6] This acting out or role playing within the text is embedded in the actual structure of the novel. To recapitulate briefly, the main narrative, Bradley Pearson's story, *The Black Prince: A Celebration of Love*, is framed by two forewords (one by the 'editor', P. Loxias, and one by Bradley Pearson himself) and by six postscripts (one by Bradley Pearson again, four by 'Dramatis Personae' and one by P. Loxias), the whole novel being, of course, Iris Murdoch's *The Black Prince*. The four postscripts by the four main (surviving) characters in Bradley Pearson's story serve not only to deconstruct Bradley's account (the contradictions remain unresolved); they deconstruct one another. Every single human viewpoint is shown to be incomplete and partial (in both senses of the word). On the other hand, no one is shown to be entirely wrong. The narrative proper works retrospectively and is itself interrupted by the narrator's reflections as he pauses to address his friend and fellow-prisoner, P. Loxias, the recipient of his story. There is therefore an important and revealing gap between Bradley the character in the story and Bradley the narrator, who is writing in prison, from a position of much greater maturity and self-knowledge; the narrator has now undergone what he describes as the purgation, the exorcism of guilt which was brought about by his trial and unjust sentence to life imprisonment. And the narrative as a whole carries an implicit commentary by the author who stands behind her narrator, a commentary which emerges through the silences, omissions and ironic doublings and coincidences in the given story.

The Black Prince is the first of Iris Murdoch's novels to deal explicitly with the limits of articulation, speech, theory, language itself, and to trace the painful tension between the author's own need for communication and her simultaneous need for self-concealment. Iris Murdoch expresses this tension early on in the novel through the eloquent reflections of her *persona*, Bradley:

Men truly manifest themselves in the long pattern of their acts, and not in any nutshell of self-theory. This is supremely true of the artist, who appears, however much he might imagine that he hides, in the revealed extension of his work. And so I too am here exhibited whose pitiful instinct is alas still for a concealment quite at odds with my trade. (p. 12)

It is a tension that Iris Murdoch dramatises in this and later novels as a male–female dialectic: here we come to the viewpoint which has been explored by Luce Irigaray, Julia Kristeva and others that discourse, for historical and cultural reasons, has been the province of the 'masculine', so that the 'feminine' reveals itself as that which subverts, interrupts and complicates discourse. In *The Black Prince* a conflict emerges between the public male voice and the private female silence that surrounds the text, or work of art. This becomes particularly evident at the end of Bradley's narrative, when Bradley comes back full circle to the question of the necessary limitations of the work of art. At the beginning of his narrative he had thought about silence as the necessary control of speech: 'I hate, in any context, an intemperate flux of words. Contrary to what is modishly thought, the negative is stronger than the positive and its master' (p. 18). But silence in this context had meant for Bradley a fastidious refusal to commit the self, to accept the necessary imperfection which comes of trying at all. (His edgy relationship with his friend and rival, the prolific novelist Arnold Baffin, is a long exploration of this fastidiousness.) Silence here seems to be thought of, in terms of Bradley's own characteristic sexual metaphors, as a virile self-containment, set in opposition to 'the intemperate flux of words'. (We may remember that this early unregenerate Bradley also hates the intemperate flux of tears.) But by the end of the novel Bradley has realised that silence is the necessary end-point of the *achieved* work of art, the commitment having been made, what cannot be said controlling what is said. Without this final surrender to the void, art is, in Bradley's words, 'a vain and hollow show, a toy of gross illusion'. Bradley continues, addressing his friend, Loxias:

> You who are a musician have shown me this, in the wordless ultimate regions of your art, where form and substance hover upon the brink of silence, and where articulate forms negate themselves and vanish into ecstasy.
>
> (p. 392)

Loxias takes up the image in the last postscript:

> That music points to silence is again an image, which Bradley used. All artists dream of a silence which they must enter, as some creatures return to the sea to spawn. The creator of form must suffer formlessness. Even risk dying of it. (p. 414)

The sexual imagery has shifted, as silence becomes the containing element. The proximity of death, the negation of form, the makeshift nature of all language, all theory, the stress throughout the novel on *tact* as necessary ellipsis and control, the disguised presence of the female author, all these are interconnected and help to shape the self-revelations of the articulate male narrator.

The stress on tact, which is after all a form of silence, is crucial. *The Black Prince* is in many ways a violent novel: it deals with violent fantasies and with sorry deeds; with a virtual rape presented as an act of passionate love, with the enactment through murder of buried jealousy and resentment in marriage. The novel is directly concerned with the libidinal energy at the base of artistic, erotic and spiritual experience, and with the potentially extremely embarrassing connections between artistic creation, erotic desire and sado-masochistic impulses. To describe *The Black Prince* in these terms is simply to invoke its explicit basis in Freudian psychology. The novel as a whole sets a serious and thoughtful reading of Freud (Bradley's many reflections on artistic creativity, for example) against the disastrous and sometimes comic misappropriations of Freud's thought in popular Freudianism (whose spokesman here is the self-appointed psychoanalyst, Francis Marloe). So, for example, Bradley's insight into *Hamlet* in the course of the tutorial which he gives Julian, 'He [Shakespeare] transmutes his private obsessions into a rhetoric so public that it can be mumbled by any child' (p. 200), has at its base Freud's famous distinction between the artist and the neurotic (*Introductory Lectures in Psychoanalysis*, 1916–7). The 'true artist', says Freud,

understands how to work over his day-dreams in such a way as to make them lose what is too personal about them and repels strangers, and to make it possible for others to share in the enjoyment of them. He understands, too, how to tone them down so that they do not easily betray their origin from proscribed sources. Furthermore, he possesses the mysterious power of shaping some particular material until it has become a faithful image of his phantasy; and he knows, moreover, how to link so large a yield of pleasure to this representation of his unconscious phantasy that, for the time being at least, repressions are outweighed and lifted by it. If he is able to accomplish all this, he makes it possible for other people once more to derive consolation and alleviation from their own sources of pleasure in their unconscious which have become inaccessible to them. . . . [7]

The problem with reductive Freudian criticism of *Hamlet* (of the sort which Bradley parodies in his tutorial) is that it seeks to do what Freud himself insisted cannot be done with works of art, to translate the public (pleasure-giving) rhetoric back into private obsessions. Exactly the same is true of Francis Marloe's comically Freudian account of Bradley's *The Black Prince*. Through Francis's gleeful tracking down of obsessions Iris Murdoch manages to parody her own complex Freudianism and also to disarm critics who might be tempted to do the same with her work. Her stance is cunning, defensive and tactful.

Throughout the novel tact is explicitly associated with irony, 'our dangerous and necessary tool'. Human experience and understanding contain deep fissures which we sense in daily life as violent and senseless clashes of perspective:

> Almost any tale of our doings is comic. We are bottomlessly comic to each other. Even the most adored and beloved person is comic to his lover. The novel is a comic form. Language is a comic form, and makes jokes in its sleep. God, if He existed, would laugh at His creation. Yet it is also the case that life is horrible, without metaphysical sense, wrecked by chance, pain and the close prospect of death. Out of this is born irony, our dangerous and necessary tool.
>
> (p. 81)

Irony, like tact, is a way of controlling violence (while fully acknowledging its horror) through the selection of an apt form (male narration and all) for the vision conveyed. This form gives the whole work its balance, its beauty; just as, in Titian's picture of the flaying of Marsyas (the myth which lies behind the novel), the radiant serenity of the composition makes the horrible suffering of its subject possible and even bearable to contemplate, opening up (as Iris Murdoch herself has shown elsewhere in her moving commentaries on the painting) a variety of possible readings, possible responses.[8]

The question then arises as to how the difficult and embarrassing subject-matter of *The Black Prince* is mediated through the male narration. Through the dramatising of the *separateness* of herself from her narrator Iris Murdoch is able to deal very intelligently with the suffering and turmoil that often underlie artistic and erotic experience and also, more obliquely, with the darker horrors of war, hunger and disease which inform human consciousness—she has Bradley reflect on this:

> That this world is a place of *horror* must affect every serious artist and thinker, darkening his reflection, ruining his system, sometimes actually driving him mad. Any seriousness avoids this fact at its peril, and the great ones who have seemed to neglect it have done so only in appearance.
>
> (p. 348)

In this passage at least we may feel that the masculine pronouns represent rather more than a (characteristically) conservative adherence to grammatical convention, that like the Bradley *persona* they are providing the author with a form of necessary protection and disguise. And through Bradley Iris Murdoch sensitively dramatises the human difficulty in adequately contemplating and responding to this violence and suffering, especially where it concerns the lives of other people. At the point of the narrative where these dark reflections of Bradley occur, Priscilla has committed suicide. The waste of her life is associated by the novelist with Bradley's generalised misery here. But Bradley is, as he well realises, incapable of dwelling very long or disinterestedly on what he comes to see at the end of his novel as the 'precise and random detail' of Priscilla's wretchedness. Instead he continually feels the reality of it slipping away even as he contemplates it.

An episode which well conveys this slipping away process occurs after Bradley has visited Priscilla's husband, Roger, and his young girlfriend, Marigold, in an unsuccessful attempt to recover some of Priscilla's 'little things' for her. Bradley is feeling for a time 'almost mad with defeat': he claims however no credit for his pity and anger; he is simply grieving for himself, he says, identifying with his sister for 'simple old mechanical reasons' (p. 109). Now he sits alone near the quay side in Bristol, before taking the train back to Paddington:

> I was looking at a ship's funnel and it was yellow and black against a sky of tingling lucid green....
> 'All things work together for good for those who love God', said Saint Paul. Possibly, but what is it to love God? I have never seen this happening. There is, my dear friend and mentor, some hard-won calm when we see the world very detailed and very close: as close and as vivid as the newly painted funnels of ships on a sunny evening. But the dark and the ugly is not washed away, this too is seen, and the horror of the world is part of the world.   (p. 108)

But as Bradley continues to 'write these words which should be lucid and filled with glowing colour' he feels 'the very darkness of my own personality invading my pen . . .'. And as he looks back from the time of his present narrating to the time of the narrated action the darkness falls and the 'empty lighted street' resembles a 'theatre set'. The insights gained fade away and a new heightened figurative style signals the blurring of moral distinction, the inevitable return to *eikasia*. At the end of the road is a ship's hull and Bradley sits on the stone quay, leaning his head against the hollow steel and revolving dream-memories of his childhood in the shop with Priscilla:

> Ships are compartmental and hollow, ships are like women. The steel vibrated and sang, sang of the predatory women, Christian, Marigold, my mother: the destroyers. I saw the masts and sails of great clippers against a dark sky.
>
> (pp. 109–10)

The style is rhythmic, incantatory, rhetorical, and signals the invasion of Bradley's pen by the darkness of his own personality. He slides here into a mode of poetic generalisation which is also a form of self-dramatisation. Priscilla disappears and the precise and random details of her wretchedness fade again out of sight. Again style and setting are beautifully framed to suggest obliquely not the dawning this time but the fading of a precious moment of insight. The way is prepared for the cruel, ironic twist at the novel's centre where Bradley's utter absorption in his love for the young Julian leads to his total abandonment of his sister, and so to her death.

But as the *persona* through which his author explores the disturbing connections between art and Eros Bradley is forced to change a good deal. At the beginning of the events related in the narrative he is almost pathologically restrained and cold. His fear of women is linked to his distaste for strong emotions and for their physical expression. This connection appears as one of the misogynist generalisations which are so characteristic of Iris Murdoch's chilly heroes:

> I cannot stand unbridled displays of emotion and women's stupid tears. And I was suddenly deeply frightened by the

43

possibility of having my sister on my hands. I simply did not love my sister enough to be of any use to her, and it seemed wiser to make this plain at once.   (p. 75)

The adjectives 'unbridled' and 'stupid' stand in apposition to one another and, together, comment implicitly upon Bradley's fastidious restraint. Of course, like other Murdochian heroes, he is educated through a series of disturbing experiences of humiliation and defeat to a point where he acknowledges in himself the attributes of 'unbridled' feeling, helplessness, loss of dignity, that he projects upon the women. Francis's postscript exaggerates the patterned, mechanical elements in Bradley's behaviour and ignores his subsequent maturation and development, but it does identify, in its crude way, Bradley's rather Sartrean disgust with women, the body, the emotions, the feminine *viscueux:*

> The female principle is what is messy, smelly, and soft. The male principle is what is clear, clean and hard. So with our Bradley. We find him gloating (I fear there is no other word) over the physical discomfiture, the uncleanliness, the ailments of his women.   (p. 397)

The relationship between the author and her *persona* is extremely complex. It is further complicated by the way in which Iris Murdoch has split her sense of her own authorship (or authority) between Bradley Pearson and his rival Arnold Baffin who is, by contrast, a prolific and successful professional writer who does not acknowledge any muse. As someone who is relatively free from egotism Arnold is well qualified to demolish various mystiques as, under pressure from Bradley, he here demolishes the mystique of 'being a writer': 'I write whether I feel like it or not. I complete things whether I think they're perfect or not. Anything else is hypocrisy. I have no muse' (p. 50). Arnold's secular and pragmatic approach is the necessary counterpart to Bradley's deepening reflections about art and his growing commitment to the spiritual and artistic goal of self-transcendence.

Through the two novelists, Bradley and Arnold (seen through the distorting medium of the jealous Bradley's narration), Iris Murdoch explores her own art with its need for partial concealment of the self. The fictionalised relationships between writer and reader contrast the deeply intimate rapport between Bradley and his reader, Loxias, with the hostile reception which Bradley as reader gives to Arnold's work. Arnold, like Iris Murdoch, commands a very wide readership and similarly confronts the uncertainties of critical reception and the inevitably mixed responses of this wide readership. Like Arnold, Iris Murdoch writes out of evident enjoyment as a writer who delights in the creation of separate, self-contained fictional worlds. But at the same time she is able to project her more personal sense of the connection between artistic, erotic and religious experience through the meditative narration of her *persona*, Bradley Pearson. In a characteristically playful aside, where she removes the mask for one moment, she has Bradley say of the artist's attempts to control the slippery, glamorous medium of language, 'What can one do but try to lodge one's vision somehow inside this layered stuff of ironic sensibility, which, if I were a fictitious character, would be that much deeper and denser?' (p. 81). Because Bradley Pearson *is*, of course, a fictitious character the ironic layers are that much deeper and denser. Behind the fiction of Bradley addressing a male friend in the novel is the fact of the female author addressing a large unknown audience who will make of her text what they choose: an audience who can be trusted only obliquely since an intimate, *tête-à-tête* relationship is not possible here. The seemingly spontaneous outpouring of memories and reflections which Bradley offers to his friend (in place of the formally perfect novel which he had spent nearly a lifetime quixotically projecting) becomes something much more probing and problematical when we posit a female author as origin of the text. It crosses gender boundaries, in particular those boundaries which normally separate male and female sexual and erotic experience. It explores areas of the psyche which are not normally accessible to us. As Bradley says, defending himself against the drastic over-simplifications of Francis Marloe, 'Of course we have an "unconscious mind" and this is partly what my book is about. But there is no general chart of that lost continent' (p. 15). The mask of the male narrator, rather like the male disguise of the heroines of Shakespearian comedy, allows the author both the pleasure of projecting herself into a dramatic role and protection in exploring difficult and dangerous regions.

A Word Child and *The Sea, The Sea* provide less complex but equally cogent versions of the male narrator. In *The Sea, The Sea* the medium is ideally suited to the personality of the narrator. As I mentioned earlier, the journal, with its double tendency towards self-justification (as an account of how the writer has chosen to spend his or her time) and self-congratulation (the self-conscious culling of 'beauties' in the recording of intense moments of aesthetic perception), is the right form for the narcissistic Charles Arrowby. But the journal he writes offers itself to be read between the lines, to be deconstructed by the sceptical reader. As Charles settles into his solitary seaside existence after his power-ridden life as a celebrated theatre director, the continual message is 'how very much I am enjoying myself here. If only . . .'. The double message may be heard in the comic disjunctions, the apparently irrelevant observations which find their way into Charles's writing, drawing attention slyly to his obsessive grudge against the past. In the following passage the paragraph-break marks an expressive pause, the censoring of a thought process:

> It is evening. The sea is golden, speckled with white points of light, lapping with a sort of mechanical self-satisfaction under a pale green sky. How huge it is, how empty, this great space for which I have been longing all my life.
> Still no letters.   (p. 15)

And in this example the logical contradiction between the first reflection and the second conveys Charles's half-conscious sense of guilt: 'The end of life is rightly thought of as a period of meditation. Will I be sorry that I did not begin it sooner?' (p. 2). A similar gap draws attention to the childhood regrets and resentments which are to surface later: 'Yes, this is my natural element. How strange to think that I never saw the sea until I was fourteen' (p. 4).

Particularly comic are Charles's records of his practical plans for improving his Eden: again they suggest the (generally human) inability to live in the present: Charles is divided from his luminous present by the very act of writing about it:

> The sunny golden rocks stand out against that dark background. What a paradise, I shall never tire of this sea and this sky. If I could only carry a chair and table over the rocks to the tower I could sit and write there with the view of Raven Bay. I must go out and study my rock pools while

this intense light lasts. I think I am becoming more
observant . . .   (p. 88)

Iris Murdoch has well caught the twistings and probings
of the restless intellect in Charles's style. In one
contemplative moment the narrator of *The Black Prince*
speaks of the 'mean and servile if onlys of a peevish
spirit' (p. 349) which can cloud our experience of
suffering; Charles provides a comic version of those 'if
onlys' which cloud the experience of joy.

Charles's journal betrays him in other ways. As he
writes his very first paragraph looking out over the sea
Charles does not realise that he is contemplating
himself. He sees the sea as 'bland', as 'cold', the depths
unillumined. Subtly his writing about it will throughout
the novel reflect his own inner states as well as what he
'sees' outside. Hence Charles's sea is a spawner of
mythical monsters. The relevance of these monsters to
his general view of human sexuality and of femaleness in
particular is obvious. Like Bradley in *The Black Prince* he
has a horror of the hidden aspects of female flesh, its
viscosity; only he does not confront this horror with
Bradley's honesty. The connections between the various
opening mouths whose pink interiors fill Charles with
nervous disgust, the mouths of his friends as they sing,
of his own sea-monster, of Titian's sea-monster in the
painting of Perseus and Andromeda, and his memory of
a bad LSD trip, with his accompanying feelings about his
own mental foulness (conveyed in the vague image of
'entrails') are complicated and implicit. The connection
between Charles's veiled sexual disgust and the self-
contempt which springs from his experience of intense
jealously is brilliantly confirmed in the detail of the
writing when Charles describes his state of mind as he is

about to spy upon his former love, Hartley, and her husband, Ben. He is approaching their house, Nibletts, and his role as voyeur makes him 'sick with emotion and terror':

> A marriage is so hideously private. Whoever illicitly draws back that curtain may well be stricken, and in some way that he can least foresee, by an avenging deity. Some horrible and quite unexpected revelation could persecute the miscreant henceforth forever with an almost obscene haunting. (p. 194)

The emotions aroused are primitive, Oedipal (their intensity suggesting the witnessing of a Freudian 'primal scene'). Again the dominant image is of something which should be hidden (the technical meaning of 'obscene') being unexpectedly revealed, as the monster's head rises above the surface of the sea.

Charles is gradually released from his obsessive horror (and its accompanying significant silences) by the bewildering twists and turns of the narrative, the events which overtake him as he writes. He is able by the end of the book to write about his most painful experience, his long-standing affair with the domineering actress, Clement, an affair which was concluded by her terrible slow death. The eerie gaps and silences in his narrative begin to disappear as by a circuitous and unexpected route he recovers something of the innocence that he originally set out to find.

In *The Sea, The Sea*, Iris Murdoch maintains a consistent and aesthetically satisfying distance from her male narrator. But in *The Philosopher's Pupil* the female author is much more elusive. The narrator, N, as he calls himself (for Nemo, No one, or indeed Narrator), is not the hero nor even, as he himself informs us, one of the significant actors in the drama. He is, he assures us, a 'discreet and self-effacing narrator' (p. 23) who knows to some extent a number of the *dramatis personae* and lives in their town to which he refers as 'N's town' or Ennistone. George refers to N on one occasion as 'that impotent voyeur' (p. 489), a phrase which parodies N's presentation of his own role and indeed that of all 'detached' narrators: 'I am an observer, a student of human nature, a moralist, a man; and will allow myself here and there the discreet luxury of moralizing' (p. 23). I think that one of the greatest problems posed by this difficult novel concerns the degree of reliability of N's narration and interpretation of the events recounted. Is he a transparent pane of glass or is he a distorting medium, a flawed reflector? How distorting is his language? Since he makes only the most teasing and fleeting of appearances it is extremely difficult to know how far to trust him. The other narrators as heroes in their drama undergo a process of education through experience and acquire an ethical perspective in which they (and the ideally wise reader as constructed through the text) can view their past selves. The ageing N emerges through his style of writing, with its circumlocutions and archaic syntax (compare the terse and witty style of Hilary Burde in *A Word Child*), as garrulous, fussy, old-fashioned, slightly pompous. He seeks continually to interpret, order, reconcile, to impose meaning. Like Jake Donaghue, he is one of Iris Murdoch's 'incurable metaphysicians', and may plausibly be seen as a scapegoat for the novelist herself, carrying her discomfiture with the novelist's voyeur-like role and her awareness that to order experience through the novel-form is inevitably to falsify it. But such an account of the relationship between author and narrator is oversimple and only partially valid.

The clue to the problems involved in N's stance is perhaps provided in the letter which he receives from Father Bernard after John Robert's death—'about what you had to say in your letter about John Robert; I believe you are wrong. You are too *interested*, it is for you a spectacle' (p. 553). N produces a virtually endless series of speculations concerning the motives of both the philosopher and his pupil. As the novel progresses there is, I think, an increasingly disconcerting gap between 'scene' and 'summary', between N's *showing* of events and his interpretation of them. This is particularly evident in his commentary upon the relationship between the philosopher, John Robert, and his grand-daughter, Harriet, in the rather jarring contrast between the taut, almost Jamesian ambiguities of the dialogue and the idle gossipy tone of N's characteristic questioning. This is nowhere more apparent than in the coda where N continues to speculate:

> I wonder (for of course I would never ask her this) whether she ever meditates upon the strange fact that it was John Robert and not Tom who first awakened her sexually. It is certainly fascinating to consider how successfully (and indeed how literally), in the end, the philosopher carried out his plan of thrusting her into Tom McCaffrey's arms.
>
> (pp. 557–8)

It is hard not to feel that N's garrulousness actually diminishes the importance of the events in the story. The same is true of N's speculations about the George/Stella *ménage* (pp. 546–8 and 555–6). The revealing comment is here: 'I find it difficult myself to leave the subject of George, whom I confess I enjoy discussing regularly with Stella.'

N lacks the wiser Murdochian narrator's awareness of

the treacherous, slippery nature of language, a sense of that point which the narrator of *The Black Prince* has increasingly in view, the point where words have to give way to silence (the limitations imposed by the muse). What is particularly interesting in *The Philosopher's Pupil* is that Iris Murdoch explicitly draws attention to the dialogue between her own offstage presence as female author and her male narrator who speaks front-of-stage. In the sly concluding paragraph N writes:

> The end of any tale is arbitrarily determined. As I now end this one, somebody may say: but how on earth do you know all these things about all these people? Well, where does one person end and another person begin? It is my role in life to listen to stories. I also had the assistance of a certain lady. (p. 558)

Here the author herself puts in a teasing appearance, rather as Elizabeth Gaskell did at the end of *Sylvia's Lovers* (1863) where a nameless 'lady' visits the 'Public Baths' and asks for information about the characters in the story. The 'certain lady' of Iris Murdoch's novel, the Muse, Murdoch herself, suggests a hidden 'M' novel behind the 'N' novel. This 'M' novel makes its presence felt, I would want to argue, precisely in the worrying discrepancies between the mysterious, frightening events described and the all-too-human reductive commentary. In his gossipy coda (which in this, in some ways very Victorian, novel corresponds to what Victorian publishers used to call the 'wind-up'), N hazards judgements, speculates about sex-lives. As Joyce Carol Oates points out in her review of the novel there is here some mockery of the puppet-master as well as of the puppets.[9] Behind the puppet-master is the 'masked presence' or 'secret voice' not indeed of one of the main characters as N reminds us (p. 23), but of the novelist herself. Her larger wisdom is felt in the silence which underlies N's loquaciousness, in the inadequacy of his judgements and in the curious left-over emotion which is generated by the novel's disturbing mixture of formally tragic and comic modes. I shall have to return to these questions in the last chapter. The nature of this dialogue between author and narrator turns out to be bound up with the problems of genre, of what kind of novel this is and how to read it, and also with the pervasive narrative symbolism which pulls against the apparent urge towards articulation, order, reconciliation and metaphysical explanation.

But I hope that I have said enough at this point to show that the device of male narration in Iris Murdoch's novels is enabling as well as disabling. It causes us to look afresh at what it means to 'write as a woman'. The American writer, Tilly Olsen, in her book *Silences* speaks of '*Casting (embodying) deepest comprehensions and truths in the character or voice of a male*, as of greater import, impact, significance' as one of the cultural distortions which mar female creativity—the temptation to 'write like a man'.[10] There is, as I have already suggested, a relatively long-established tradition of feminist criticism which broadly supports this view. But Iris Murdoch's novels can be seen to throw this assumption into question, as they do so much else.

53

Chapter Three

Degrees of Confinement: The Plots and the Settings

It is now time to turn to the other side of the question, to the 'absence of a corresponding female voice'. While the articulate hero sets out on his imaginary quest the silent heroine too often languishes in the prison-house of the Murdochian plot. My previous chapter implicitly posed the question of what happens in the other novels, the novels which do not employ a dramatised narrator but rely instead on a blend of ominiscient and third-person centre-of-consciousness narration. I shall put forward some necessarily brief suggestions about the modes of narration in these other novels.

The term 'voice' suggests better what Iris Murdoch is doing with her language than does the traditional word 'style', which implies a consistency or evenness in the tenor of what is *written down*, a consistency which is notably missing in Iris Murdoch's writing. Elizabeth Dipple's helpful drawing of attention to the 'complex and shifting voice' in Iris Murdoch's narration[1] describes, I think, the experience of reading the novels more accurately than A.S. Byatt's admittedly acute analysis of 'how good and bad prose can occur on the same page'.[2] But it is A.S. Byatt's comment that has apparently set the tone of most of the reviews of the later novels. One reviewer of *The Philosopher's Pupil*, for instance, distinguishes between a 'cold' style (N's archaic, precise narration) and 'a "hot" style which seems to come unbidden to the characters at certain moments' and clearly dislikes the latter (the well-known Murdochian eloquence).[3] But what he does not go on to say and might have done is that, given that the 'cold' and the 'hot' styles belong to different voices within the narrative (in this case to N and to George), they have different functions and, as I have suggested in the last chapter, the clashes, the contradictions between different voices, different discourses, have ultimately the effect of emphasising the provisional, incomplete nature of the narrative.

A plurality of 'voices' can also, as I indicated in the last chapter, be discovered within the single voice of the dramatised narrator. So Bradley in *The Black Prince* moves between a rather deadpan colloquial appraisal of facts and a heightened figurative mode which is characteristically a form of self-deception. The examples showed how the modulations in voice can take place in the course of a single sentence, the modulations corresponding beautifully to shifts in the narrator's perception of himself in relation to his surroundings and to other people.

The selection of a 'voice' seems for Iris Murdoch to be bound up, above all, with her grasp of a particular *relationship*. For this reason it seems to me that the novels where she does employ a dramatised narrator are, on the whole, more satisfying as literary *texts* than are the others, which are sometimes marred by passages of unpersuasive omniscient narration. In these passages we again encounter the author's habitual though intermittent uncertainty about how far to collude with or to detach herself from the perspective of her characters. Sympathy and irony tug in opposite directions, and a curious vagueness or self-absenting results (the central flaw, as I saw it, of *The Italian Girl*). The absence of a dramatised narrator exposes this uncertainty. A single example may help to show what I mean.

In *An Unofficial Rose* (1962) the impersonal narrator describes Ann Peronett's brief and uncharacteristic revolt against her fairly unhappy marriage: 'Ann felt within herself the blissful stir of a selfish will. She welcomed it as a mother might welcome the first moment of her unborn child' (p. 282). The concluding simile here poses a problem. It is both over-obvious and curiously irrelevant. After all Ann *is* a mother and furthermore she happens at this moment to be getting the worst of a conversation with her 'difficult' daughter, Miranda. The authorial subjunctive 'as a mother *might* welcome . . . ' is incongruous and detracts from the dramatic significance of the scene; the vagueness here reflects the author's uncertain relationship with her character. This is one of the moments where she does not fully 'inhabit the action', and the style registers the lack of authority.

The problem seems to arise where the author wishes to convey inarticulate or half-articulated emotional states which she characteristically seeks to convey through the consciousness of the women in her novels. The gulf between her men and her women is well shown in her many descriptions of falling/being in love. While her male characters tend, rather comically at times, to reach for their Plato, her female characters have recourse instead to the poignantly inadequate clichés of magazine romance. So the widowed Mary Clothier in *The Nice and the Good* (1968) muses upon her unrequited love for Willy:

> Then she thought, is this really all I have to look forward to, is that what I have to comfort myself with? Years more of managing someone else's house and then a job as a school teacher? But my wants are huge, my desires are rapacious, I want love, I want the splendour and violence of love, and I want it now, I want someone of my own. Oh Willy, Willy, Willy. (p.106)

The plight of the woman condemned to mere usefulness, living in someone else's house, has been explored profoundly by women novelists from Jane Austen onwards. Here the treatment is glib (to say the least) and the prose reduces Mary's predicament to the level of magazine cliché. This must surely be, according to any traditional criterion of literary merit, the worst-written paragraph in the whole Murdoch cannon, but the 'lapse' is significant. The omniscient authorial comments which follow Mary's reflections are of a piece with this, in their almost defiant parade of clichés:

> Yet she knew that it was not really the sharp tragic knife of passion that disturbed her now, it was some vaguer nervous storm out of her unsatisfied woman's nature. The dreariness was already with her, it had its part in her present jumpiness, her present tears. (p. 108)

The narrator's 'she knew' appears to endorse Mary's self-belittling and detached comment on her 'woman's nature'.

It is tempting at this point simply to write off Mary Clothier as someone her author isn't much interested in.

But Mary's reflections appear in an interesting new light if we read them in the context of the immediately preceding narrative, the opening of the chapter in which they occur. This new perspective is centred upon the presence of a 'minor character', the disgruntled Irish housekeeper, Casie:

'They treat women properly in Russia,' Casie was saying as she removed the pudding plates. 'In Russia I could have been an engine driver.'

'But you don't want to be an engine driver, do you?' said Mary.

'Women are real people in Russia. Here they're just dirt. It's no good being a woman.'

'I can imagine it's no good being *you*, but—'

'Oh do shut up, Theo.'

'I think it's marvellous being a woman,' said Kate, 'I wouldn't change my sex for anything.'

'How you relieve my mind !' said Ducane.

'I'd rather be an engine-driver,' said Mary crazily.

Casie retired to the kitchen.   (pp. 103-4)

The conservation, unremarkable in itself, is, in the light of the plot and dramatic situation, a subtle and oblique commentary upon the power relationships which link the characters. The emotionally greedy Kate is happily content with the maternal/seductive image which she presents for her retinue of men; she does not need to question herself or her gender identity. Ducane, in love with Kate, and lover of a much younger woman whom he patronises and dominates, does not want at this stage to hear of women's dissatisfaction with the status quo either in this household or in society in general. (In the light of this conversation it is one of the felicitous ironies of the plot that he should eventually marry Mary.) Casie, useful, teased and largely ignored, *is* dissatisfied and searching for a way of expressing that dissatisfaction. Her reference to Russian engine-drivers is comic and provokes some smiling but the comedy does not undermine either her dignity or her point of view. Interestingly, her own predicament in this selfish household finds its echo in Mary's; Mary too feels herself to be merely useful. Her sympathy with Casie leads her to take up the image of engine-driving, and the 'craziness' which she is associated here reveals the crack or craze in her own consciousness of herself—her horror of a gender role which can in this house, so it seems, only exercise any power in the fundamentally dishonest, emotionally greedy way in which Kate exercises it—in being, in short, as Kate is, all things to all men.

Mary's subsequent magazine-style reflections upon her own emotionally deprived state are illumined by the immediate context, with its glimpse of the fissure, the crack in her self-perception. Powerless as she is, she falls back on stock romantic notions of an ideally fulfilling passionate love, a love which she focuses upon a man who cannot reciprocate it.

In this novel as in others the author seems to be experimenting with different kinds of discourse, different ways of codifying the experience of 'being in love'. The magazine romance offers one kind of discourse, and this may carry an authorial sense of how women in her society, having, in general, fewer outlets than men for self-realisation, are more likely to have recourse to simplifying and consoling fantasies.[4] But the Platonic discourse of the male characters has its own pitfalls as a way of sustaining romantic illusion; Miles in *Bruno's Dream* (1969) and Charles in *The Sea, The Sea* both confidently misappropriate it to justify their experience of a love which proves in the event to be fundamentally self-regarding. In *The Nice and the Good* and its immediate successor, *Bruno's Dream*, there arises a third, eclectic, discourse which draws upon various meditative texts— Plato, the Bible, Simone Weil and, more immediately, the author's own philosophical writings—to convey a sense of love as seen in the perspective of death.[5] Significantly, Mary moves from her stock romantic clichés to a moving meditation upon what the narrator calls later, in a haunting phrase, 'the other face of love, its blank face' (p. 350), as she waits almost without hope for the return of her own son and John Ducane from their shared ordeal in Gunnar's Cave; her thoughts come to us mediated by the eloquence of the impersonal narration:

> Death happens, love happens, and all human life is compact of accident and chance. If one loves what is so frail and mortal, if one loves and holds on, like a terrier holding on, must not one's love become changed? There is only one absolute imperative, the imperative to love: yet how can one endure to go on loving what must die, what indeed is dead? . . . Since death and chance are the material of all there is, if love is to be love of something it must be love of death and chance. This changed love moves upon the ocean of accident, over the forms of the dead, a love so impersonal and so cold it can scarce be recognized, a love devoid of beauty, of which one knows no more than the name, so little is it like an experience. This love Mary felt now for her dead husband and for the faceless wraith of her perhaps drowned son. (pp. 309–10)

The clumsiness of Mary's reflections on Willy at the earlier point in the narrative is, as the context reveals, closely related to her feelings of powerlessness and failure. In general terms the absence of a female voice to correspond with the highly developed male narrational voice has some disturbing implications in Iris Murdoch's fictions.

She continues to place her women in the most unhappy predicaments. Her tight love-plots rarely work in favour of her female characters. Whereas for the men in love the women may indeed embody the force of the contingent, the accidental and the unexpected (this is particularly true of *Henry and Cato* (1976) with its reflections on the power and unpredictability of 'goddesses', as Lorna Sage has well shown),[6] for the women the experience of 'love' very often comes as a defeat. Sometimes it spells actual imprisonment in the Gothic mode where women are shut up in houses by fathers/lovers/husbands as is Hannah in *The Unicorn*, Elizabeth in *The Time of the Angels*, Dorinda in *An Accidental Man*, Hartley in *The Sea, The Sea*. Often the female characters are shown as enslaved in relationships to selfish men who like to keep them in 'cold storage': Georgie in *A Severed Head*, Adelaide in *Bruno's Dream*, Jessica in *The Nice and the Good*, Emily in *The Sacred and Profane Love Machine*, Diane in *The Philosopher's Pupil*. Together with Iris Murdoch's large cast of unappreciated female domestics (from the Italian Girl herself onwards) they are shown living in houses (or apartments) where they do not really belong, where they have no rights. The men, on the other hand, even when as impoverished as is the priest, Cato (*Henry and Cato*), lay claim to their 'place' with a certain degree of self-confidence.

Even where marriage and/or property offer a degree of security the loss of an adequate sense of self, often epitomised by a failure to cultivate an artistic talent, reveals itself in a semi-conscious unease within the confines of the house. Harriet in *The Sacred and Profane Love Machine* (1974) is relatively undisturbed by her 'aching sense of a tiny lost talent' (p. 16), an epitaph for too many female artistic hopes in Iris Murdoch's fiction, but for Alex McCaffrey in *The Philosopher's Pupil*, awareness of 'what she thought of as her career as a failed painter' gives rise to veritable hauntings, to a kind of 'animism' which afflicts many of the female characters: 'Alex's quickening of the world about her was neurotic and corrupted, the final distortion of those artistic impulses with which she had so irresolutely played' (p. 63). And Harriet's unconscious knowledge that her marriage is failing manifests itself in a similar unease: a compulsive collecting of stray dogs and a persistent fear of burglars. Hood House becomes for Harriet a confining fortress in which she strives to maintain a sense of security.

The plots, the structures in which the female characters find themselves are shaped by the dialectic played out in the novels between constraint (the bonds of love being hard to loose) and freedom with all its ambiguities. For the women (fragilely inserted as they are into the symbolic order) freedom is a condition which hovers precariously between a discovery of new, more personal and demanding connections with the world and others (as Anne Cavidge finds in *Nuns and Soldiers*) and a collapse of the self into moral and psychological chaos (the fate of Morgan in *A Fairly Honourable Defeat*). Harriet in *The Sacred and Profane Love Machine* is fairly caught between conflicting demands of love and freedom when she is driven out of the narrow sphere where she has been happy to live. (Her violent and accidental death at Hanover airport reflects a final closing of options.) The habit of loving, of needing particular connections, proves to be too strong for Harriet: she suffers intensely towards the end from a moral and emotional agoraphobia. Between the extremes of agoraphobia and claustrophobia Iris Murdoch's women appear to find little resting-place.

The question now arises as to what this preoccupation with thwarted and confined women reveals about Iris Murdoch's fiction-making process in general. In a group of novels dating from the early 'sixties, from *The Unicorn* (1963) to *The Time of the Angels* (1966), this preoccupation amounts to near-obsession. The fiction in this respect is interestingly illumined by the relative simplifications of Iris Murdoch's work for the theatre.

In the two plays originally conceived for the theatre and written slightly later than this group of novels, *The Servants and the Snow* (1970) and *The Three Arrows* (1972), the plot-structure and setting seem deliberately chosen to reflect patriarchal structures at their harshest and most archaic. So *The Servants and the Snow* takes place in an old isolated country house in winter, where the masters of the quasi-feudal community have re-established the ancient *droit de seigneur*: the right to sleep with their vassals' brides on the wedding-night. The play opens when the new master, Basil, arrives on the death of his father to take over the vast estate and rather more than two hundred servants. Basil is most discomfited to learn that his ancestors, his father included, practised the *droit de seigneur* and that this quasi-magical exercise in power lies behind the mysterious cohesion of the feudal community. It is through this exercise in power that Basil's father was able to preserve his authority in the wake of a dreadful crime (he murdered one of his servants out of desire for the servant's wife, Marina). Basil in his attempt to establish a liberal regime precipitates a crisis of power in which his authority and his life are under threat. It turns out (of course) that the only way Basil can re-establish his authority is by himself exercising the *droit de seigneur* with regard to Marina, who is now marrying for the second time. This Oedipal plot also functions as an obvious political allegory on the fate of modern liberalism and capitalism in a small revolution-torn (Balkan?) state.[7] Basil's liberal government fails: he is undermined not only by the feudal traditions which he is powerless to alter but also by the threat of anarchy (represented by Patrice and the gipsy community). The play ends with a military coup as General Klein, Basil's brother-in-law, turns up at the last moment to restore order and the status quo. Basil has, meanwhile, been assassinated by his outraged wife with a shotgun.

In *The Three Arrows*, a much subtler political study, the setting is the Imperial Palace in medieval Japan, where the women are sequestered in their own quarters. The opening stage direction for Act I, Scene iii, conveys the nature of this imprisonment eloquently enough:

> The apartments of the princess. Afternoon. A latticed window makes the room curiously reminiscent of YORIMITSU'S cell. Rocks, stones, dwarf trees, sand, etc., ingredients for making a miniature garden, in the foreground. . . . As the stage lightens AYAME is playing the zithern. The music stops. Silence. Atmosphere of female ennui.

While the youthful princess Keiko yearns for love, but principally for more *space* (she has never been outside her father's palace), her attendant, Koritsubo, is disillusioned, resigned to staying put. 'Women have to stay in the same place mostly. It may as well be a nice place. . . . We are women. They make our lives miniature', and so on. But the scene, and the play in general (rather like the previous play where there is much talk of women's political situation), does not feel very urgently concerned with the women's lot. The sheer prettiness of the scene takes the sting out of Koritsubo's disillusioned commentary. The closing stage direction suggests an unconscious irony on Iris Murdoch's part: 'The yellow winter light, the snow, the three girls at the lattice, make a pretty picture.' The *detachment* here is borne out by the very structure of the play; it is virtually split between the all-male scenes and the all-female scenes while the dramatic interest is focused upon the men. The drama of *choice*, the choice among the three arrows of the title (the paths of love, action and holiness), belongs to the political prisoner, Yorimitsu. Keiko shows initiative, romantically taking on male disguise to further her love for Yorimitus, and stabbing herself at the end of the play. But her self-sacrificial act is a *result* of the choice made by Yorimitsu, and stabbing herself at the end of the play. Keiko reacts, rather than acts.

Like the two plays, the 'Gothic' novels, from *The Unicorn* to *The Time of the Angels*, convey a slightly chilly detachment towards the female characters on the part of the female author. It is as if she were seeking to conjure up and exorcise uncomfortable feelings about female imprisonment/oppression by simultaneously dramatising and distancing these feelings through the device of centring the story upon acts of male choice. In these archaic worlds, as in the historical novel, *The Red and the Green* (1965), male and female spheres of action are rather ruefully shown as sharply divided, linked only by the demands and vagaries of erotic love.

The 'Gothic' novels, *The Unicorn, The Italian Girl, The Time of the Angels*, offer what are in a sense visions of hell, taking place 'in camera', where taut and terrible family relationships are played out in terms of diabolical triangles, all doomed repetitions of the original Oedipal drama. (In this respect the list may be extended backwards to include *A Severed Head* (1961) and the more sober *An Unofficial Rose* (1962).) The daughter-figure in these dramas is in love with her father, or (in a variant of the pattern) with the same man as her mother (as are Miranda in *An Unofficial Rose* and Flora in *The Italian Girl).*

Of these novels perhaps the most eloquent and disturbing is the last, *The Time of the Angels.* It concerns, in part, the fate of Muriel Fisher, daughter of the Rector, Carel. Carel resembles the 'doubly-fathered father' in Judith Wilt's description of the Gothic mode in that he is both father and priest.[8] Muriel and her half-sister Elizabeth are, like the typical Gothic heroine, motherless. The novel as a whole has been much criticised for its patent contrivance but a careful reading shows, rather, how Iris Murdoch is concerned to treat certain kinds of socially and culturally induced female misery here, as elsewhere, within carefully established limits. Her use of such authorial devices as male narration, multiple and elaborate plot-structures, Gothic setting and mythological frameworks allows her to write of these experiences with a certain control and detachment. The elaborate plot-structures, in particular, serve to protect both author and her readers against the intensity of feeling which she so characteristically evokes, as becomes obvious if we slow the reading process down for a moment. So, for example, we see Muriel pass into a state of complete psychic inertia after Pattie's revelation of the true relationship between Carel and Elizabeth. Muriel is hopelessly entangled in the incestuous web of her relations with her father and half-sister and cannot bring herself to stir from the house and from the father who has rejected her. She passes a period of time 'lying upon her bed in a state of coma':

> The intense cold seemed to dim and lower her consciousness until there was nothing except a faint flickering awareness which was scarcely aware of itself. Something lay upon her, pinning her to the bed.... The little daylight

went soon and darkness came. Time passed. Footsteps passed. A light turned on in the corridor shone in through the half-open door of the room. But nobody came to her. Pattie did not come. Carel did not come. And Elizabeth did not ring her old familiar bell. The house fell silent. (p. 203)

Muriel struggles against this 'extinction of the will' in attempts to move her painfully alienated body and to leave the house. But her will fails her as her very identity is bound up with the house and its occupants: 'Here was the stuff she was made of and running away could make no difference' (p. 204).

However, Muriel's state of mind is not dwelt upon long enough to become deeply painful to the reader; the plot twists yet again as Carel's unexpected suicide initiates the final stage of the drama and then the reader is propelled into the more comfortable, and saner, consciousness of Carel's brother, Marcus. And similar techniques are used to distance the not dissimilar miseries of Dorinda Gibson Grey and Charlotte Ledman in *An Accidental Man* (1971).

These depictions of confined women significantly recall the poems of Tennyson, that connoisseur of psychological paralysis. The two most 'Gothic' novels, *The Unicorn* and *The Time of the Angels*, with their persistent images of bowers, mirrors and tapestries, recall Tennyson's 'The Lady of Shalott' but pose the question, as Tennyson's poem does not, of why the lady was imprisoned in the first place. And in a way these veiled references to Tennyson's text are a comment on the male tendency to 'textualise' the woman, to reduce her to text or to myth, a process that Iris Murdoch's rehandling of the vocabulary of courtly love, the woman as *princesse lointaine*, enchantress and Lilith, comments upon with more direct and obvious irony. And one may

Iris Murdoch

see in the description of Charlotte Ledman's depressive
state (*An Accidental Man*) images which are wryly
reminiscent of Tennyson's 'Mariana in the Moated
Grange'. The detail of the 'buzzy blue flies' and the
very Tennysonian handling of the pathetic fallacy
suggest that Charlotte's Angelo, like Mariana's, will
never come:

> Her loose tooth was aching. The sun was shining into the
> kitchen and on to a number of opened and half emptied tins.
> There was a smell of decay and a quantity of buzzy blue
> flies. Charlotte wandered out of the kitchen again and into
> the bedroom which faced north. The bed was unmade. . . .
> She lay down on the bed.   (p. 295)

If Iris Murdoch *as* author inevitably colludes, to some
extent, in the male process of 'textualising' the woman,
shutting her up in words, images and fictive houses, she
is at any rate able to comment intelligently on her
collusion, as she does through the consciousness of
Muriel in *The Time of the Angels*, meditating upon
Elizabeth's confinement:

> why did she suddenly think of it all as a diabolical plot? If it
> was a plot it was one with which she had herself long
> cooperated. She had never challenged the view that
> Elizabeth was ill and needed to be protected from the shocks
> of the world. She herself had been Elizabeth's chief
> protector from those shocks. She herself had made, and
> made with deliberate care, the bower in which Elizabeth
> now seemed so alarmingly drowsy and entranced. It had all
> seemed necessary.   (p. 132)

And Iris Murdoch shows how in imprisoning Elizabeth
Muriel in effect imprisons herself. At the climactic

moment of the narrative, gazing into the depths of the mirror in which the act of incest is reflected, Muriel achieves simultaneously a process of painful self-realisation; she becomes herself a Lady of Shalott and succumbs to Elizabeth's own living death.

At an important moment in the narrative Muriel, confronting her father, experiences the 'drowsiness' which she attributes to Elizabeth, and with it a terror of 'an isolation, a paralysis of the will, the metamorphosis of the world into something small and sleepy and enclosed, the interior of an egg' (p. 131). The world which closes in on Muriel is a nightmare of the abuse of patriarchal authority.

Is it, then, to take up a point which I made earlier, this dread of such states of moral and psychological stagnation which impels the Murdochian plot on its breakneck career of surprising reversals and dramatic dénouements in a courageous re-assertion of the comic vision of life? Certainly in the light of the novels of the mid-'sixties, with their atmosphere of physical and psychological claustrophobia, the development of Iris Murdoch's later fiction can be appreciated afresh. The broadly comic structures of the later novels seem in part designed to assure the characters that they do indeed have a future (as the ageing Hugh Peronett in the early *An Unofficial Rose* was delighted to learn) and that the future holds surprises. It should be stressed, however, that there is no process of simple wish-fulfilment at work. Charlotte (*An Accidental Man*) can in her suicidal state conceive of no future that is not 'a series of nightmarish rat-run extensions of her present vileness' (p. 297). She proves to be wrong, but the surprising future in store for her, life in a country cottage with failed athlete, Mitzi, the woman who after a series of comic mishaps and coincidences becomes her lover, is to be fraught for Charlotte with emotional ambiguity and she in fact finds herself regretting her lost solitude with characteristic bitterness.

In general, the opening out of the plot-structures brings with it a liberation of the female characters as they become free to evaluate for themselves the often conflicting claims of self and others, and also, significantly, to find ways of communicating with one another. Although a novel as late as *The Nice and the Good* (1968) can present an almost ludicrously formalised scene (Chapter 14) where the three central women in the story, Paula, Mary and Kate, walk along the beach 'in single file' without exchanging a single word, each woman self-absorbed, meditating upon her relationship with a particular man, the later novels do go on to explore, with increasing depth and flexibility, the inter-relationships among the female characters. The tight love-plots are loosened as the claims of female friendship, itself often obliquely erotic, are seen to weigh more heavily in the balance: thus, for example, Anne and Gertrude in *Nuns and Soldiers* (1980) and Hattie and Pearl in *The Philosopher's Pupil* (1983).

This process may be very briefly illustrated by noting Iris Murdoch's treatment of her stock wife and mistress confrontation in three successive novels, *A Severed Head*, *The Sacred and Profane Love Machine* and *Nuns and Soldiers*. In the first of these the confrontation between the wife, Antonia, and the mistress, Georgie, catches beautifully the contrast between Antonia's nervous and unintentional condescension and Georgie's stubborn and graceless honesty. But no communication between the two is possible (partly because they are so conscious of being observed by Martin). Wife and mistress remain locked within the stereotypes of the domestic triangle.

In *The Sacred and Profane Love Machine* the two central

female characters, the wife, Harriet, and the mistress, Emily, are rather spoilt by the highly conventional terms of their initial presentation (seen as they are largely through the consciousness of the husband/lover Blaise): Harriet, 'chaste modest virginal' (p. 83), Emily, dark and demonic. The gulf between the two women is formally echoed throughout the narrative in various ways: in the novel's rather Blakean 'London', split into prosperity and deprivation, into north and south of the Thames, and in the divided psyches of its different characters, in the undermining of their conscious moral attitudes by various dreams and hauntings. Of course the dualities are set up to be (partly) collapsed, although Harriet's naive urge to reconcile and contain the opposites proves to be in the end disastrous, and the surviving characters (apart, perhaps, from Edgar) settle more or less happily for a diminished, one-sided existence.

The first meeting between Harriet and Emily is a moment where the stereotypes which conceal the female characters are suddenly undermined and the narrative undoes its own cynically dualistic terminology. Emily, unlike Georgie, has the authority to send her lover out of the room so that she confronts Harriet alone in a tense moment; the moment proves to be one of those disconcerting shifts of perspective (or 'switches of *gestalt*') which Iris Murdoch is so good at describing:[9]

Years later Emily McHugh still remembered this moment with the greatest clarity. It was a moment of revelation, when deep feelings, which have seemed leaden and immovable, suddenly begin to skip like the mountains of the psalmist, and intellect, like a flash of lightning, reveals a completely new configuration. Briefly put, Emily realized that she could not hate Harriet. At any rate, she realized that 'the hated wife' was over and done with and some quite different problem had come into being.   (p. 156)

Part of the interest of this passage is the way the narrator appears to be revising her own assumptions together with her character ('Briefly put . . . at any rate') while her metaphor of the shifting landscapes of the mind illumined in sudden flashes uncovers the metaphors hidden in such unclear and unrevealing terms as 'clarity' and 'revelation'. The sudden dissolving for Emily of set assumptions about 'wives' and 'mistresses' prepares the way for a brief period of communication between the two women before the barriers of class and status separate them again. In their next meeting, this time on Harriet's territory, they exchange banalities over drinks; their words and actions rigidly determined by their relationship to the central male character, Blaise.

Nuns and Soldiers (1980) gives its female characters a new freedom of thought and action. The domestic triangle reappears but only to be broken open. The part of the wife, Gertrude, is displaced on to her close friend, Anne, who acts as self-appointed agent in Gertrude's interest when she seeks out Tim's mistress, Daisy. Their meeting is ostensibly a disaster but at the same time the two cannot help liking each other. Daisy's extraordinarily comic ability to disconcert her gentle interlocutor by mistaking all the cues and upsetting the conventions of polite social intercourse recalls the less well-developed but also very funny dialogue between the elderly suffragette, Camilla Wingfield, and the well-bred Rosa in *The Flight from the Enchanter*. That Anne maintains a warm interest in Daisy and that these two sympathetically drawn and temperamentally opposed women share a destiny of sorts, both going to America to different kinds of 'sisterhood', Anne to the Poor Clares in Chicago, Daisy to a community of feminist friends, indicates how much less Iris Murdoch is now inclined to confine her women within the structures of the traditional erotic plot.

The 'latest Iris', *The Good Apprentice* (1985), provides ample evidence of Iris Murdoch's extraordinary ability to undo her own patterns, while simultaneously recalling them. For instance, the triangle created by marital infidelity appears yet again but, significantly, here the deceiver, the two-timer, is the woman, Midge. And this time the erotic tangle is represented with extraordinary fidelity through Midge's meandering yearnings, hesitations and regrets. In the tacit drawing together of wife and husband at the end of the novel the question of who is to forgive whom is no longer relevant.

However it must be admitted that the author's treatment of Midge in the largely masculine world of *The Good Apprentice* does once again express an ambivalent attitude towards her female characters and their experiences. Midge is small-scale: again, the mode of narration half deliberately diminishes her and suggests a rather uncertain relationship between author and character:

> Oh for freedom, to be out of this cage of lies and pain at last! She looked into her dressing-table mirror, at her beautiful hair and her distorted face, and for a moment opened her eyes wide and resumed her old insistent animated look which said 'like me, like me'. And was it she, whom everybody liked and petted, who was soon to cause such grief, such scandal and such chaos? She turned away from the mirror. (pp. 203–4)

A similar though much subtler ambiguity can be discerned in the impersonal narration which mediates the experiences of Dora in the much earlier *The Bell* (1957). As this novel is so very interesting to look at from a female-centred perspective I shall conclude this chapter and open the next with a fairly lengthy discussion of it.

Dora is the first of Iris Murdoch's confined female characters to effect her escape as she learns to become 'what she has never been, an independent grown-up person' (p. 302) and wins an economical and psychological independence of both her husband and her lover. But Dora is a creative presence in the book by virtue of what she is as well as what she is becoming. She arouses a variety of disturbed responses in the other characters. For the youth, Toby, who is attracted to her, her feminine helplessness and ignorance of everything mechanical are 'perfectly captivating' (p. 211); for the homosexual Michael, on the other hand, she is irritatingly frivolous, to begin with, and he sees her as epitomising 'everything he didn't care for about women' (p. 128). She does not escape the satire of the omniscient narrator who seems at times to comply with Michael's view of her, speaking of her 'self-conscious feminine twittering' (p. 128) and, a little unkindly, noting her twirling of her parasol as she asks sentimentally, 'Why can't the animals all be good to each other and live in peace?' (p. 123).

But despite the feminine ploys to which she continually resorts as a way of winning affection or approval Dora is said to possess, even in Michael's view, a 'naïve vitality' (p. 121) or a *native* vitality which is an invigorating force throughout the book. This vitality stands in contrast to the rigidly masculine demeanour of Dora's academic husband, Paul. Paul lives by the values of single-mindedness and self-discipline, qualities which might be admirable if he did not put them to purely egotistical use. Paul's desire for offspring says everything about his position as a representative and agent of patriarchy (he is the very embodiment of Lacan's 'symbolic order'!):

> The sense of family was strong in him and he preserved an ancestral nostalgia for the dignity and ceremonial of kinship. He yearned for a son, a little Paul whom he could instruct and encourage, and finally converse with as an equal and even consult as a rival intelligence. (p. 10)

It follows that motherhood would have improved Dora's status in Paul's eyes, as the narrator points out: it 'would have invested her no doubt with some impersonal significance drawn from the past. But Dora had no taste for such genealogical dignities. . . .' Dora has remained paralysed in her dealings with Paul up to this point so that she is totally unprepared for children and yet doesn't make any effort to prevent conception.

It is perhaps not over-fanciful to see in Dora certain analogies with the female text as described by Cixous, Irigaray and Kristeva: like the female text Dora subverts patriarchal, logical expectations, possesses a multitude of meanings, and is characterised by the presence of *jouissance*, female pleasure. This is nowhere more apparent than in Dora and Paul's contrasting attitudes to 'work'. Paul applies himself to his studies with an admirable single-mindedness but his passions ultimately serve his ego. Dora has no such 'work' in which to lodge her self-esteem. (The female household tasks at Imber appear irksome to her until she gets the power to run the place herself and to carry out these tasks in her own way.) But at the end of the book she returns unexpectedly to her long-neglected painting and creates a series of watercolours of Imber. She has no desire for success; she is not concerned with her talent or lack of it but paints out of sheer joy.

It seems that her own creator feels uncomfortable with her at times, and the omniscient viewpoint has a tendency to shade into Michael's: 'he was well aware that James had been right in calling her a bitch and that it was unlikely that her career of crime was at an end' (p. 304).

This is chilly indeed; no other character, not even Paul, is so harshly judged. Again we encounter the split attitude which is at the heart of Iris Murdoch's treatment of female experience. It is an ambiguity which, as I have indicated, is closely bound up with the author's selection of a 'voice' and with her handling of impersonal narration. It continues to haunt her work.

Chapter Four

The Sibyl's Cave:
Narrative Symbol

'We live in myth and symbol all the time', Iris Murdoch
has remarked in a review.[1] She admits furthermore to a
personal myth which informs her work, but we can
ultimately only guess at its outlines.[2] In this chapter I
wish to look at some ways in which Iris Murdoch uses
her dominant narrative symbols to explore the resources of her creativity as female writer. Again we shall
see how the writing can be read (in Elaine Showalter's
terms) as 'a double-voiced discourse, containing a
"dominant" and a "muted" story, what Gilbert and
Gubar call a "palimpsest" ' where 'The orthodox plot
recedes, and another plot, hitherto submerged in the
anonymity of the background, stands out in bold relief
like a thumb print.'[3]

The presence of such a feminist subtext can be
discerned throughout *The Bell* where Iris Murdoch's
narrative symbolism is particularly sustained and subtle.
In this connection I would like to explore two of the
symbols whose full significance only emerges out of a

reading of the whole narrative—the fruit garden at Imber, and the bell itself.

The fruit garden is described in a fine passage of complex and unobtrusive symbolism. It is worth quoting in full. (Mrs Mark is conducting a rapidly wilting Dora on a tour of Imber's activities on a particularly hot summer day):

She pushed open a heavy wooden gate in the wall and they came into the fruit garden.

The old stone walls, dry and crumbling with the long summer, covered over with brittle stonecrop and fading válerian, enclosed a large space crammed and tangled with fruit bushes. A wire cage covered an area in the far corner, and there was a glint of glass. A haze hung over the luxuriant scene, and it seemed hotter than ever within the garden. Disciplined fruit trees were spread-eagled along every wall, their leaves curling in the heat. Dora and Mrs Mark began to walk along one of the paths, the dried up spiky fingers of raspberry canes catching at their clothes.

'Why, there's Catherine', said Mrs Mark. 'She's picking the apricots.'

They came towards her. A large string net of small mesh had been thrown over a section of the wall to protect the fruit from the birds. Behind the net Catherine was to be seen, almost lost in the foliage of the tree, dropping the golden fruit into a wide basket at her feet. She wore a floppy white sun hat under which her dark hair straggled in a long knot, hazy with wisps and tendrils, which hung down between her shoulder-blades. She was intent on her labour and did not see Dora and Mrs Mark until they had come very close. Her dark head, thrown back beneath the powdery glow of the hanging apricots, looked to Dora Spanish, and again beautiful. Her averted face, without the nervous self-protective look which it wore in company, seemed stronger, more dignified, and more sad. Dora felt that strange misgiving once more at the sight.

78

'Hello, Catherine!' said Mrs Mark loudly. 'I've brought Dora to see you.'
Catherine jumped and turned about, looking startled. What a jittery creature she is, Dora thought. She smiled and Catherine smiled back at her through the net. (pp. 71–2)

The fruit garden suggests both a medieval *hortus conclusus* and a Renaissance Eden, and in it Catherine is figured obliquely as Persephone, or indeed Eve. The passage is rich in Miltonic and Marvellian overtones. The evocation of the laborious discipline through which the natural luxuriance of the garden is both protected and held in check, the spread-eagled fruit trees, the raspberry canes which catch at the clothes, the exotic apricots and the mesh recall the gardens of Marvell. Catherine herself is seen like Milton's Eve in terms of the luscious vegetation which surrounds her as she works with it; her hair like Eve's with its wisps and tendrils is suggestive of the profusion of nature. The market garden partakes of the almost indefinitely extensive and subtle symbolism which characterises so much of *The Bell*. For the less imaginatively susceptible members of the Imber community it functions as a place of honest practical labour with measurable economic returns, a means to self-sufficiency. But here, with Catherine at its centre, it suggests the erotic energies which the community will find so hard to hold in check. It comments proleptically upon the appalling consequences that will follow from Catherine's attempt to discipline her own sexual nature through her choice of the religious life, an attempt in which all the members of the lay community are implicated.

But a further range of significances emerges if we read the passage from a female-centred perspective.

79

Catherine is here seen through the eyes of another woman and this is crucially important to the relationship between this passage and the narrative as a whole. The relationship between Dora and Catherine is one of potentially great sympathy but it is given little chance of development. The shy attempts of the two at communication are continually interrupted by the brashly insensitive Mrs Mark (as in this episode) or by Dora's possessive and domineering husband, Paul. There hovers over the narrative the sense of a narrowly missed happier outcome to Catherine's story, an outcome that might have been realised had Dora managed to reach her.

In this passage the details of Catherine's dress and stance suggest a romantic pastoral heroine, which is how she appears to the still somewhat jealous Dora (Dora would like to be just such a figure herself but totally lacks the necessary dignity). So Dora's reaction to her first glimpse of Catherine had been

> an immediate twinge of displeasure. She realized that she had been assuming that if she had to decorate so uncongenial a scene she would at least be the only beautiful girl upon it. A woman of the appearance of Mrs Mark was quite in place here. (p. 31)

But she moves quickly from a position of wry self-conscious rivalry to a complex mixture of emotions when Mrs Mark tells her, just after the conclusion of the long passage quoted above, that Catherine is going to join the enclosed order of nuns in the Abbey. Dora experiences a horrified surprise, relief, pain, pity and also 'some terror, as if something within herself were menaced with destruction' (p. 73). Dora's half-conscious yearning for the spiritual peace which the community represents for her, even though she feels so out of place in it, links her with Catherine, as Catherine's half-conscious desire for sexual and emotional fulfilment links her with Dora. But this second half of the equation is present only as guesswork for the reader, who is not allowed into Catherine's consciousness. Dora is the only character who shows any interest in what Catherine's state of mind might be.

There is a sense in the above passage of how the rigid divisions which human beings impose upon labour as well as love can cause creative exuberance to ebb away. Dora's entry into the fruit garden follows on from the ominous as well as very funny words of Mrs Mark:

> 'We believe that women should stick to the traditional tasks. No point in making a change just to make a change, is there? We'd be so glad if you ever felt like joining in any time. I expect you're handy with your needle?'
> Dora, who was not, was feeling the sun extremely.
>
> (p. 71)

Mrs Mark's inane pieties with the oppressiveness of her repeated 'we', the heat of the day, Catherine's dignified sadness and Dora's obscure terror all suggest the tension and unease within the comedy. An obliquely conveyed sense of oppression, of thwarted female potential, hangs over the scene.

The tentative sympathy between Dora and Catherine, the possibility, never fulfilled, of a friendship which is much needed by both, goes completely unrecognised by the other members of the community. The narrative itself does not emphasise it. But the Dora/Catherine story forms an important subtext to Michael's long, sad failure to find ways of communicating with Mick Fawley, Catherine's brother. The female subtext, with its stress on sympathy and practical help, offers some obliquely illuminating contrasts to the main story and makes a feeling contribution to the novel's exploration of different kinds of isolation within community.

A 'Dora-centred' perspective can also enrich our response to the central symbol in the novel, the bell. The symbol has been criticised by A.S. Byatt as the only flaw in an otherwise excellent novel. Her argument is long and complex but may be summed up in her own words, taken from the pamphlet for the British Council:

> its moment of action, when Dora rings it, is a substitute for a real action in the real world inhabited by the characters. Dora beats it to 'tell the truth'—but the truth she has to tell has nothing to do with the bell. The connexion is the novelist's.[4]

The bell is what A.S. Byatt in *Degrees of Freedom* calls a 'planted' symbol; it has been consciously placed there by the novelist to convey a general statement of truth. As such it contrasts with the 'natural' symbol, 'something real in an action or a piece of fictional scenery, to which certain emotions quite naturally attach themselves, even in terms of the characters' own perception of them'.[5]

The argument in both of A.S. Byatt's studies is interesting and indeed persuasive but leaves, I think, something out. The 'connexion' between truth-telling and the ringing of the bell is, after all, Dora's, as well as the novelist's. The ringing of the bell is only one of a number of *consciously* symbolic actions which Dora takes in an attempt to resolve her predicament in relation to her husband who doesn't respect her and to the Imber community by whom she feels casually judged. One such moment is her action of throwing her lipstick out of the window in an attempt to disturb the reflections in

Imber Lake. Dora's 'fit of solipsistic melancholy' is externalised in a brief and memorable description:

> The sun was shining, the lake was hard and full of reflections, the Norman tower presented to her one golden face and one receding into shadow. Dora had the odd feeling that all this was inside her head. There was no way of breaking into this scene, for it was all imaginary.
>
> (p. 182)

Dora's sense of alienation from her own body (Paul's love-making that morning had left her feeling 'tired and unreal') as well as from her surroundings (she has no real context in the Imber community) is well conveyed as the still and picturesque landscape becomes a disconcerting mirror of her bewildered emotional state. Time has been stopped dead in its tracks. An idea occurs to Dora of 'trying somehow to break into the idle motionless scene'. But her symbolic attempt fails, the object she finds to throw, her lipstick, vanishes 'falling presumably far short of the lake, somewhere in the long grass' (p. 183). Dora, feeling 'almost tearful', then decides to take the train back to London.

Dora's later idea of raising the old bell buried in the lake and secretly substituting it for the new bell at the ceremony which will admit Catherine to the Abbey is a similar though more violent symbolic act of self-assertion. And Dora's converse action, her ringing of the old bell so as to give away her powerful secret and thereby forestall its potentially harmful consequences (p. 267), is yet another self-assertive act at a much deeper moral level. Dora refuses any longer to 'play the witch' or to make the bell her 'plaything'. But it may be noted that the act still satisfies Dora's baser motives by making her the centre of attention as the others crowd round her, summoned by the urgent deep booming of the bell.

It is *after* this theatrical act, this quite crude way of forcing the others to take full account of her presence, that Dora's relationship with everyone else in the community starts to change. She watches the ceremony of the next day with a growing involvement and concern which culminate in her attempt to rescue the despairing Catherine from the lake, and in her final making of her own terms with Imber. Her early attempt to disturb the hard reflections of the lake had failed but her later breaking into the scene, the unsettling of what she sees as Imber's casual judgement on her (its hard reflections?), is obliquely realised in the ringing of the bell. The action is theatrical, symbolic, cathartic.

The bell itself changes its significance as symbolic object according to the characters who respond to it. James and Michael appropriate the new bell as religious symbol in their sermons. Although they use it in opposite ways to support their opposing religious ideals they both consciously use the bell to mean only one thing. But for Toby and for Dora the old bell itself is a symbol of a more elusive and less conscious kind. For Toby with his personal experience of raising the old bell from the depths of the lake, the bell's retrieval functions as a rite of passage, linking youth to young manhood, school to university, (sexual) ignorance to (sexual) knowledge. For him the bell is associated with Dora and its gradual recovery with his growing sense of intimacy with her (p. 215). But it is in connection with Dora that the mysterious significance of the bell fully emerges. When Dora is left alone with the old bell she is impressed and frightened by its physical presence:

It was black inside and alarmingly like an inhabited cave.

Very lightly she touched the great clapper, hanging
profoundly still in the interior. The feeling of fear had not
left her and she withdrew hastily and switched the torch on.
The squat figures faced her from the sloping surface of the
bronze, solid, simple, beautiful, absurd, full to the brim
with something which was to the artist not an object of
speculation or imagination.   (p. 267)

The bell is threatening because it expresses by its history,
its function in the narrative, and its very shape the
inescapable connections between erotic and spiritual
love. The imagery throughout this section is powerfully
erotic as well as religious; it links the bell with
unexplored and unexpressed (female) sexuality as well
as with the spiritual energy of the past which speaks to
the present through carvings and inscription in a foreign
and only half-understood language. The writing itself
here emphasises the connection which all the characters
(except for the Abbess) seek in their different ways and
for their different reasons to deny, with all the unhappy
consequences.

All the symbols in the narrative seem to reach their
emotional as well as their logical fulfilment in the
presence of the naively vital Dora, whom her author has
described in a luminous phrase as 'a painter and a child'.[6]
Accordingly, as Dora rows alone across the lake,
crossing for the last time those symbolic waters
which separate the house from the Abbey, the
narrator reminds us implicitly that she has learnt
to swim: 'The depths below affrighted her no
longer' (p. 316). The sentence draws its full range
of meanings from a knowledge of the entire preceding
narrative with its insistence upon the image of
hauling up unknown hideous/beautiful objects out
of the depths.

I'm arguing that a 'Dora centred' perspective allows

for a more flexible and emotional reading of Iris Murdoch's symbolism in *The Bell* than does a 'neutral' overview. It allows us in Elaine Showalter's phrase to see 'meaning in what has previously been empty space'.[7] From here it is possible to argue that Iris Murdoch's symbolism in general presents a 'double-voiced discourse'.

To illustrate this, I will turn to a consideration of what is perhaps the most complex and interesting symbol in Iris Murdoch's writing, the symbol of the Cave. The primary reference is, of course, to Plato's parable of the Cave as a metaphor of the human condition of *eikasia*, subjection to shadowy illusion. It may be useful at this point to summarise Plato's parable which I will do by quoting Iris Murdoch's own account in *The Fire and the Sun:*

> The prisoners in the Cave are at first chained to face the back wall where all they can see are shadows, cast by a fire which is behind them, of themselves and of objects which are carried between them and the fire. Later they manage to turn round and see the fire and the objects which cast the shadows. Later still they escape from the Cave, see the outside world in the light of the sun, and finally the sun itself. The sun represents the Form of the Good in whose light the truth is seen; it reveals the world, hitherto invisible, and is also a source of life.   (p. 4)

But Iris Murdoch characteristically deflects and alters the significance of those philosophical statements and metaphors which she inscribes into her narrative. As Alasdair MacIntyre has pointed out in a perceptive review, 'Iris Murdoch's novels are philosophy: but they are philosophy which casts doubts on all philosophy including her own.'[8] Her practice is the patient deconstruction of assumed truths. It is not surprising therefore that the Cave, itself an image of illusion, should have in her narratives its dark and mysterious double as a site of potential truth, the Sibyl's Cave.

The Platonic parable of the Cave has itself been important to much feminist critical enquiry. As women we are in the situation succinctly described by Adrienne Rich of 'reading the Parable of the Cave/while living in the cave'.[9] Gilbert and Gubar have extensively considered the ways in which women writers have revised Plato's parable. The Cave is, after all, '—as Freud pointed out—a female place, a womb-shaped enclosure, a house of earth, secret and often sacred'.[10] By figurative extension (as one of the symbolic *loci* associated with Jung's maternal archetype) it suggests female space, creativity and power. It carries all these associations in the legend of the Sibyl who dispensed from her cave an archaic wisdom in scattered leaves. Gilbert and Gubar ask accordingly:

> How ... does any woman—but especially a literary woman, who thinks in images—reconcile the cave's negative metaphoric potential with its positive mythic possibilities? Immobilized and half-blinded in Plato's cave, how does such a woman distinguish what she is from what she sees, her real creative essence from the unreal cutpaper shadows the cavern-master claims as reality?[11]

This very question has been explored in a dazzling piece of metaphorical virtuosity by Luce Irigaray in her *Speculum, de l'autre femme* in which she sees Plato's Cave as a metaphor, or metaphorical process, which has underlined the course of Western metaphysics.[12] The Cave stands in this masculine representation for the womb, the matrix, also the earth. It is described as a *theatrical* enclosure (*enceinte théâtrale*)—where the representations, the images proposed by the inherent metaphoricity of

Western thought are deployed. These images are distorted, reflecting the tendency of metaphor-dominated discourse to translate sexual difference into a series of hierarchically organised oppositions (woman becomes man's shadow, or mirror-image). The Platonic image of the Cave proposes a set of oppositions, differences, discontinuities between outside and inside, high and low, daylight and earth-fire, escaped man and prisoner, truth and shadow, truth and veil, reality and dream, the intelligible and the sensible, good and evil, the One and the many. These oppositions, Irigaray goes on to say, 'always assume a *leap* from worse to better. An ascension. A displacement (?) towards the heights, a progression along a line. Vertical. Phallic?'[13] In this leap the possibility of negotiation, trans-ition, moving to and fro between these two realms is forgotten. The misleading topography of the Cave-as-womb leaves out, ignores, the corridor, passage or link between the Cave and the outside world, the 'forgotten vagina'. The Cave as the site of difference is negated by the single principle of the divine paternal logos envisaged in the parable as the Sun.

It is impossible here to do justice to the complexity, the brilliant perversity, of this re-reading of Plato's parable. What Luce Irigaray has done is to reverse in minute detail the nexus of metaphors present in the parable to show their applicability to the privileging of male systems of representation in Western philosophical discourse. So in her re-reading, for example, the sun/logos, the dazzling of the Good, the mirage of the Absolute, blinds the man who gazes upon it so that in his return to the cavern of his past he will see nothing. The path to the sun has led to loss of vision.

Speculum, de l'autre femme, like other female re-writings of Plato's parable, throws unexpected light on Iris

Murdoch's ambiguous contrast between Cave and Sun. We may, for example, see a curious and suggestive parallel between Luce Irigaray's image of the blinding sun of the paternal logos with the *'hysterical* blindness' which George McCaffrey suffers at the end of *The Philosopher's Pupil* after his prolonged contemplation of the 'sunflower sun'. This is the culmination of George's search for redemption in his pursuit of his erstwhile teacher, the philosopher, John Robert Rozanov, a man with whom he is obsessed. Rozanov continually rejects George, partly, we are led to believe, through his own loss of faith in philosophy and partly through what Iris Murdoch has described in an interview as his hatred of 'messy and emotional situations'; a repugnance which spills over into his human relationships from his philosophical work, with its demand for 'perfect truth'.[14] George's quest leads him to his temporary blindness, as in a crazed state, after his apparent murder of the philosopher, he stares at the sun, the Platonic image of truth. Under his gaze the sun turns into a terrifying image of destruction:

> It was no longer round but was becoming shaped like a star with long jagged mobile points which kept flowing in and out, and each time they flowed they became of a dazzling burning intensity. The star was very near, too near. It went on flaming and burning, a vast catastrophic conflagration in the evening sky, emitting its long jets of flame. And as it burnt with dazzling pointed rays a dark circle began to grow in its centre, making the star look like a sunflower.
>
> (pp. 539–40)

This passage has a gentler, comic equivalent in the very first of the novels, *Under the Net*, where Dave Gellmann's method of teaching philosophy is described. The young students, says Jake, are 'natural metaphysicians' aspiring to the truth 'like sunflowers', something that Dave who deals in his 'own particular brand of analytic linguistic philosophy' regards with disgust. The sunflower image is unobtrusively picked up as Jake goes on to say of *this* philosopher's relation with his pupils: 'He blazes upon them with the destructive fury of the sun, but instead of shrivelling up their metaphysical pretensions, achieves merely their metamorphosis from one rich stage into another' (p. 25).

Iris Murdoch's most sustained fictional re-working of the parable of the Cave is to be found in *The Sea, The Sea*. Charles appropriates it in an extensive passage:

Since I started writing this 'book' or whatever it is I have felt as if I were walking about in a dark cavern where there are various 'lights', made perhaps by shafts or apertures which reach the outside world. (What a gloomy image of my mind, but I do not mean it in a gloomy sense.) There is among those lights one great light towards which I have been half consciously wending my way. It may be a great 'mouth' opening to the daylight, or it may be a hole through which fires emerge from the centre of the earth. And am I still unsure which it is, and must I now approach in order to find out? This image has come to me so suddenly, I am not sure what to make of it. (p. 77)

Charles remains uncertain as to what to make of this image of the Cave for the rest of his journal. 'I remember', he says at the beginning of his journal, 'James saying something about people who end their lives in caves. Well, this, here, is my cave' (p. 4). It is the opening of a new life which is designed to be innocent and secluded; Charles has chosen to 'abjure magic and become a hermit' (p. 2).[15] The Cave is associated here with Prospero's cell where the truth may be learnt and

where the illusions of power (the illusions of the theatre)
are finally relinquished. But is Charles's cave to be a
Cave of illusion or a cell of truth? With an inward-
turning movement which is characteristic of this witty
novel where the outside turns out to be the inside (and
vice versa) the Cave in the passage I quoted earlier turns
into an image of Charles's own mind, not where he is,
but what he is.

The author plays ironically with Charles's version of
the parable. Hartley, the object of Charles's obsessive
love, is the Platonic sun to which 'All the best, even
Clement, have been shadows by comparison' (p. 77), and
Charles proclaims a little later, 'The light in the cavern is
daylight, not fire' (p. 79). But Charles continually revises
and reverses this apparently confident judgement. And
in the end the parable itself is revised and reversed by the
author. The apertures to Charles's cave multiply in
a bewildering way and truth becomes increasingly
hard to distinguish from illusion. A slightly wiser
Charles, in the last of his many reflections on Hartley,
settles eventually for a partial truth, an incomplete
illumination:

> One can be too ingenious in trying to search out the truth.
> Sometimes one must simply respect its veiled face. Of
> course this is a love story. She was not able to be my
> Beatrice nor was I able to be saved by her, but the idea was
> not senseless or unworthy.   (p. 500)

The image of respecting the 'veiled face' of truth notably
undoes the truth/veil dichotomy that Luce Irigaray sees
in the parable of the Cave, just as the whole novel
questions the outside/inside dichotomy and, by extension, the other hierarchical oppositions implied
within the parable. Irigaray's feminist re-reading of
Plato turns out, unexpectedly, to illumine Iris Murdoch's.

The Cave in *The Sea, The Sea* is both the theatrical enclosure in which we live and a place of contemplation, of confrontation with inner truth, a testing-place. In several of the other novels it acts (like the original Sibyl's Cave with its labyrinth at Cumae)[16] as a transforming vessel, a place of initiation, figurative death and rebirth for the young heroes who enter it. In *The Philosopher's Pupil*, Tom, the youngest of the three McCaffrey brothers, descends as far as he can towards the source of Lud's Rill, to the underground circular space which houses the base of the elaborate workings of the Institute Baths. The journey serves his need for 'some sort of symbolic or magical act which concerned or touched his situation without running any danger of changing it' (p. 503). Even more dangerous is the adolescent Piers's (again) self-imposed ordeal in Gunnar's Cave (*The Nice and the Good*) where, in the grip of his unhappy love for the equally immature Barbara, he plans to sit out the duration of a tide. His plan becomes an obsession that he cannot explain; 'It was certainly connected with Barbara, but it might be truer to say that the idea of the cave had swallowed up the idea of Barbara' (p. 228). For both Tom and Piers the entry into the hidden place of danger brings with it a strong sensation of sexual desire. Their ordeals, like Toby's raising of the bell, act obviously as rites of passage, initiations which prove the heroes worthy of their beloveds and enable them to gain their hearts' desires—yet another variant on the quest motif.

These set pieces, however, do come across as over-contrived, their symbolic function (especially in *The Philosopher's Pupil*) apt to become tediously explicit. But they do restore the 'positive mythic possibilities' of the Cave, reclaiming it as a site of potential truth.

The woman's experience of the Cave is subtler and

more problematical in Iris Murdoch's fictions for in going into the Cave she confronts herself; in an important sense she is the Cave. So Dora experiences a complex and disturbing sense of identification with the mysterious bell, to her the bell appears 'alarmingly like an inhabited cave' (p. 267). For Iris Murdoch's confined women, whom I discussed in the last chapter, the cave is suggested by the houses which prove so terrifyingly to be extensions of their own personalities, even their own bodies. But for Anne Cavidge in *Nuns and Soldiers* who has learnt during her long years in the convent to live as if she had no body, the search for a home, a 'cell' (p. 110) leads her to confront again the experiences of living as a female body.

Fruit garden, bell, cave and sea are all part of a nexus of images which seems to be intimately associated with the author's own sense of her female artistic creativity. These images form a series of mysterious *loci* which always carry a strong libidinal charge, evoking as they do the unconscious sources of artistic and erotic creativity. The mysterious circular pool in *Nuns and Soldiers* is clearly such a *locus*. This pool whose waters seem to quiver 'in perpetual occult donation and as perpetual renewal' (p. 159) recalls the magical *puits* of Celtic legends and medieval French romances. The feckless and happy vagabond-painter Tim Reede discovers the pool near Gertrude's French house in a tenderly evoked landscape 'not quite in Provence'. He shows a fairy-tale chivalric respect for the 'crystal pool' by deciding not to bathe in it, not to 'interrupt its sibylline vibration' with his 'gross splashing' (p. 160). Gertrude, however, is able to bathe there with perfect decorum.

The many descriptions of the pool as something numinous, 'almost radiant with its own light,' recall in their evocation of beauty, autonomy and otherness the

vision of the flying saucer which more or less concludes
The Nice and the Good:

> The shallow silvery metal dome glowed with a light which
> *seemed to emanate from itself* and *owe nothing to the sun,* and about
> the slim tapering outer extremity a thin line of lambent blue
> flame rippled and leapt. It was difficult to discern the size of
> the saucer, which seemed to inhabit *a space of its own,* as if it
> were inserted or pocketed in a dimension *to which it did not
> quite belong. In some way it defeated the attempt of the human eye to
> estimate and measure.* It hovered in its *own element,* in its *own
> silence,* indubitably physical, indubitably present and yet
> *other.*   (p. 352, my italics)

Perhaps it would be too neat to suggest a parallel
between Iris Murdoch's imaginative writing here and
the lyrical and often exhilarating attempts of Luce
Irigaray and other radical French critics to evoke the
repressed 'feminine' in discourse.[17] Nevertheless, in the
light of these attempts, the phrases which I have
italicised acquire a new richness of figurative meaning.
They point to an 'elsewhere' conceived as lying beyond
the bounds of traditional philosophical discourse with its
attempts to estimate and measure, its single solar light
of reason.

Perhaps the doubleness inherent in Iris Murdoch's
treatment of the Cave as world symbol and female
symbol has something to do with the ambiguities with
which her work on Plato concludes:

> Sophistry and magic break down at intervals, but they
> never go away and there is no end to their collusion with art
> and to the consolations which, perhaps fortunately for the
> human race, they can provide; and art, like writing and like
> Eros, goes on existing for better and for worse.[18]

The Sibyl's Cave: Narrative Symbol

Richard Todd comments:

> It is significant that many readers and reviewers of *The Fire and the Sun*, while commending its lucid exposition of Plato's thought, were uncertain to what extent Murdoch was refuting or sympathizing with it, and were able to note how fascinating she found the paradoxical coexistence of puritan and artist in Plato.[19]

The image of the Cave is taken up in Iris Murdoch's moving yet ambiguous defence of art: the work of art may be in danger of becoming a Cave of illusions but its 'pierced nature . . . its limitless connection with ordinary life, even its defencelessness against its client, are part of its characteristic availability and freedom' as 'the most educational thing we have'.[20] And as a Cave of sorts, a 'theatrical enclosure', a 'theatre of shadows', to appropriate Irigaray's phrases, it allows the female author to explore, as she cannot do in her philosophical texts, her own sense of the 'free ambiguity of human life' into which the statements made by art escape, for 'Art cheats the religious vocation at the last moment and is inimical to philosophical categories.'[21] She is able to explore these ambiguities through her symbolic stage-properties and flamboyant, theatrical, symbolic gestures.

So we can discern in Iris Murdoch's novels a dialogue between the public 'male' philosophical voice and the private 'female' poetic voice. The poetic voice surprises the listener by subverting the assumptions so carefully established by the philosophical voice.[22] Its power to unsettle lies behind the often haunting and suggestively 'feminine' symbolism and is beautifully conveyed by a few brief sentences from the work of a male critic, Walter Allen's *Tradition and Dream*. These refer to a moment in *The Bell* where the absent-minded Dora, who is being berated as usual by her husband Paul, unexpectedly releases into the sunlight a Red Admiral butterfly which she had rescued from the dusty floor of her railway compartment and then forgotten about. Walter Allen quotes the conclusion of the passage, where the butterfly emerges: 'It circled them for a moment and then fluttered across the sunlit platform and flew away into the distance. There was a moment's surprised silence' (p. 25). He comments:

> The passage astonishes, enchants, liberates and enhances. It tells us, in the simple juxtaposition of Dora and butterfly, more about Dora than any amount of description or psychoanalysis could; and what it tells us is something we could learn in no other way.[23]

In its liberating and enhancing symbolism and in its subtle yet insistent feminism *The Bell* still remains unsurpassed by Iris Murdoch's later fiction.

Chapter Five

Making an Exit:
Closures and Conclusions

In *The Sea, The Sea* Charles Arrowby talked memorably about his experience of putting on plays: 'perpetual construction followed by perpetual destruction . . . endings . . . partings . . . packings up and dismantlings' (p. 36). Charles always speaks of 'dismantlings' with a certain tension and excitement: he uses the word several times throughout his narrative, in the description of his first night in the open where the continually shooting stars suggest the crumbling and dismantling of the heavens themselves (p. 145)—a vision which later leads to a memory of the 'magical Odeons' of his childhood (p. 475)—and when he thinks of his dead cousin, James, whom he loves belatedly, and whose flat which provided the memorable setting of their encounters is perhaps soon to be 'dismantled like an Aladdin's palace' (p. 498). The words 'dismantling', 'dismantled', convey the ambivalent excitement which Charles finds in the life of the theatre; they also suggest, more darkly, the necessity of endings in the world outside the theatre, associated as they are in context with the deaths of Charles's father and of James, and with Charles's own need to let go, to relinquish his jealous grip upon his past.

This awareness of the need for dismantlings informs Iris Murdoch's endings of all her novels, as she deliberately dismantles her fictional worlds. Her endings reflect, I think, her own modest and unassuming personality as a writer: she offers her novels for instant consumption, and seems in interview almost reluctant to reclaim them, once she has given them over to the public. In this she is rather like her own character, Hugo Belfounder, in *Under the Net*, who turns his enormous talents to the creation of fireworks, and, in particular, 'set pieces':

> The peculiar problems of the set piece delighted Hugo and inspired him: the trigger-like relation of the parts, the contrasting appeal of explosion and colour, the blending of pyrotechnical styles, the methods for combining *éclat* with duration, the perennial question of the coda.   (p. 55)

These are, figuratively speaking, questions which delight the novelist, Iris Murdoch. And, interestingly, what pleased Hugo most about fireworks, according to Jake, was their impermanence:

> I remember his holding forth to me once about what an *honest* thing a firework was. It was so patently just an ephemeral spurt of beauty of which in a moment nothing more was left. 'That's what all art is really', said Hugo, 'only we don't like to admit it. Leonardo understood this. He deliberately made the Last Supper perishable.'   (p. 55)

But in one of those highly comic Murdochian reversals,

Hugo gets taken up by the newspapers when the critics, delighted to discover this new genre, begin to classify his work into 'styles'. (This is not the first ironic reversal which Hugo experiences; the firework business starts in the first place when Hugo, an ardent pacifist, inherits an armaments factory.) Rather like Hugo, Iris Murdoch seeks a certain self-effacement in her work. The famous 'page-turning impetus' (to use Elizabeth Dipple's phrase)[1] which results from the strongly involuted plotting, the continual surprises, actually prevents a first-time reader from paying attention to the local dramatic strengths: the moments of extreme tension between characters, the sharply focused detail of the settings, the ways in which the language reflects psychological shifts of awareness. These can only be seen fully if the reading process is slowed down or even halted for a moment.

The 'perennial question of the coda' which so clearly fascinates Iris Murdoch is connected with the tendency of her fictional worlds to explode or dissolve just before the novels end. The undermining of whatever realist illusion remains is present in the penultimate twist or turn of the plot where effects of probability or of *vraisemblance* are completely abandoned. So in Honor Klein's return in *A Severed Head*, and Lisa's to Danby in *Bruno's Dream*, we have to do with structures of wish-fulfilment rather than the probabilities of realist fiction. In Kitty's death at the end of *A Word Child* the effect of double coincidence strains the credibility of the fiction but emphasises the question of forgiveness, and redemption of the past, which has been central to the novel. The doubleness is felt at the end of *Nuns and Soldiers* where Anne, like Daisy, projects a journey to the New World and so exits from the novel's central stage which is here (as characteristically) represented by London.

Another typical Murdochian ending is that of *An Unofficial Rose* where a sudden discovery throws a questioning, even cynical, light upon the events of the whole novel; so Ann painfully discovers that her teenage daughter is in love with the man she herself loves, Felix Meecham. No doubt the reader can here think of plenty of other such improbable penultimate twists where the overall effect is a deliberate and disconcerting distancing of the fictional world. To work the theatrical metaphor once again, the house-lights are turned up while the play on stage is still in the process of ending. The conclusion is deliberately over-emphasised in a way which destroys the novel as *eikon*, or as *fetish* (to use the Freudian term). In that sense the author modestly stresses its imperfection, that is, its incompleteness, and its defencelessness before its consumer, into whose general experience of life it is to become absorbed.

I now wish to concentrate for a while upon the moment of closure itself, where the play on words, the shifting between literal and metaphorical significance, undermines the realist illusion still further. This truly poetic stress on closure through the nuance of verbal detail is well illustrated in two of the early novels, *The Bell* and *The Time of the Angels*. Dora in *The Bell* leaves the pastoral, almost timeless, world of Imber for London. The Imber community has been disbanded; the house itself is soon to be absorbed into the Abbey, and therefore to become invisible to the outside world. Dora sees the empty windows as 'a little dark and blank, like the eyes of one who will soon be dead' (p. 316). The use of the simple future tense here comes as a surprise; strict grammatical logic would lead us to expect the future conditional, 'one who would soon be dead'. For a moment, Imber merges with the house of fiction, the novel itself, now just about to end, to 'die'. For the reader, shutting the book, the novel begins to vanish in a long perspective: 'in this moment, and it was its last moment' Imber belongs to Dora; the novel belongs in its last moment to the reader who is now in mental possession of 'the whole story'. So Dora in the last sentence of the novel looks forward to 'telling the whole story to Sally'.

Like *The Bell, The Time of the Angels* ends with the image of the deserted house, again the setting for violent actions and unexpected dénouements. The final image is of a shell, a husk of meaning, and powerfully yet unobtrusively conveys a sense of the novel's vanishing as it is consumed, the text's giving place to the new texts which the reader's own experience will create out of it, texts unguessed at by the author:

> The house had become a vacant shell whose significant spaces would soon be merged into the empty air. It would soon exist only in memory. . . . It seemed unreal, vivid and yet not truly present, like a coloured photograph projected in a dark room. (p. 216)

> The old fear would fade, and the love would fade too or else unrecognizably change. The relentless vegetable vitality of human life would grow in this case as in all others to eclipse the dead. (p. 217)

This image is particularly apt for it is linked historically to the passing away of pre-war London in the rapid destruction and reconstruction of the 'sixties. The Wren tower, rendered unsafe by bomb damage, is in the process of being demolished as the house is deserted, furniture gone, girls gone, Leo gone, Eugene sorry to leave, the house 'deathly now that it was empty' (p. 222). Marcus turns from its now-empty spaces to 'the gay

din of ringing voices and babbling transistor sets'
(p. 221).

The Unicorn gestures self-consciously towards metaphors of theatrical closure with a similar movement, as
Effie's meditations round things off:

> He was the angel who drew the curtain upon the mystery,
> remaining himself outside in the great lighted auditorium,
> where the clatter of departure and the sound of ordinary
> talk was coming now to be heard. He sighed again and
> closed his eyes upon the appalling land.   (p. 270)

Effie closes his eyes and the image vanishes. The illusory
nature, the contrivance of the fiction, is admitted in the
language which restores the fairy-tale images of
Hannah as sorceress, Lilith, enchantress: 'Hannah had
claimed her last victim' (p. 269). The novel becomes
'story': 'It had been a fantasy of the spiritual life, a story,
a tragedy. Only the spiritual life has no story and is not
tragic' (p. 268).

The framing effect in all these novels is self-
consciously theatrical; Dora, Marcus and Effie are left
over to speak the epilogue, to dismiss the audience,
reminding them that it is only a 'play'. (Here as
elsewhere Iris Murdoch offers a sophisticated rework-
ing of Shakespearian conventions.) The later novels
bring about the effects of closure more subtly; they rely
less on the set-piece, the visual image, than on the local
effects of verbal echo and allusion. So in *The Nice and the
Good* (that curiously transitional novel) closure is much
more persuasively implied (with the characteristic
gesture of dismissal) by the self-consciously literary,
oblique allusion to *A Midsummer Night's Dream*—a genial
but distancing comment on the various couplings with
which the novel concludes: 'The apricot moon shone and

the night owl hooted above the rituals of love' (p. 343)—than by the set-piece of the flying saucer's appearance.

Shakespearian echoes and allusions are obviously present in *An Accidental Man* where a cocktail party character's reference to *The Tempest*, 'Our revels now are ended', effects a momentary and magical pause in a seemingly endless kaleidoscopic round of social gossip which gives the impression of going on beyond the conclusion of the novel on paper. The 'facts' of the ending are obscured, diffused through the process of rumour into a number of partly true, partly false, versions, again cheating reader-expectations. (The fates of many of Iris Murdoch's characters are given only in gossip versions.)

The ending of *The Black Prince* makes a more subtle and oblique reference to a Shakespearian text as the editor and last speaker, Loxias, aspires to a conclusive and 'universal' statement:

> Art is not cosy and it is not mocked. Art tells the only truth that ultimately matters. It is the light by which human beings can be mended. And after art there is, let me assure you all, nothing. (p. 416)

The text closes on the word 'nothing'. Shakespeare's Hamlet asks Horatio to 'report me and my cause aright' (Loxias initially sees his task as that of a Horatio), but Hamlet himself moves out of the tightly plotted, closed structure of his life into death: 'The rest is silence.' The controlling presence of Iris Murdoch as author may be felt in the marked disjunction in tone and register between Loxias's closing of the novel proper here and Bradley's closing of his own narrative at the end of his postscript (the first of the six postscripts). Bradley does not aim at grandiloquence or generalisation: his concluding remarks are indefinite, inconclusive, almost random. He recalls three of the most important relationships of his life, with Loxias, with Priscilla and with Julian, but the words of his last paragraph show him deliberately rejecting the perfection of a formal closure. The whole paragraph is full of afterthoughts, and of approximate expressions, 'somehow', 'on the whole', 'sometimes', as the nature and significance of past experience continue to shift and elude definition. Bradley as author does not attempt to 'knit up the precise and random detail' of 'his' characters' lives. He undoes at the end his own pattern-making as he moves towards death.

The Sea, The Sea is the novel in which the author most notably undercuts her own eloquence, leading her audience to re-examine the human desire to find patterns in fiction as well as in other areas of experience. The structure of this novel is dominated by what Elizabeth Dipple calls its 'meandering refusal of closure'.[2]

This openness of the structure is reflected in the language, and nowhere more notably than in the opening to the postscript, 'Life Goes On', which occurs comically after all the devices suggestive of literary closure have been exploited. Here Charles's voice at last merges imperceptibly into the author's and so conflates the distinction between the dramatised and the omniscient modes of narration:

> That no doubt is how the story ought to end, with the seals and the stars, explanation, resignation, reconciliation, everything picked up into some radiant bland ambiguous higher significance, in calm of mind, all passion spent. However, life, unlike art, has an irritating way of bumping

and limping on, undoing conversions, casting doubt on solutions, and generally illustrating the impossibility of living happily or virtuously ever after; so I thought I might continue the tale a little longer in the form once again of a diary, though I suppose that, if this is a book, it will have to end, arbitrarily enough no doubt, in quite a short while.

(p. 477)

In the second of these two sentences Iris Murdoch playfully undercuts her own eloquent style along with the human need for conclusions. The first sentence transposes to an ironic key the Murdochian sentence with its love of adjectival fullness and its yearning reaching out towards the plenitude and detail of the sensory world. The second sentence openly mocks this mode: as, hilariously, it is unable to end; there is no arching lyrical cadence but rather 'a bumping and a limping on' and a slow grinding to a halt. The contrast between the first and the second sentence expresses, I think, everything that is most important about Iris Murdoch's use of language. On the one hand, the strengths of this style might be described in part (generalising from the examples I have given throughout this study) as a subtle and unobtrusive use of sustained metaphor, a playful use of verbal echo and repetition over varying stretches of both dialogue and descriptive narrative, and the attunement of degrees of rhetoricalness to the psychological and moral condition of the character under consideration. On the other hand, deliberate lapses appear when the author wishes to draw attention to the makeshift quality of the structures, literary, philosophical and social, in which we place so much faith.

In this context, the very last sentence of *The Sea, The Sea* is particularly thought-provoking: Charles notices with irritation that James's mysterious casket has been knocked off its bracket by hammering going on next door: 'The lid has come off and whatever was inside it has certainly got out. Upon the demon-ridden pilgrimage of human life, what next I wonder?' (p. 502). The question provides a fitting image for the imaginative curiosity which the author shares with her readers and which looks forward to the next experience of writing/reading. As Lorna Sage has observed: 'None of her novels dwells exhaustively on its subjects, or on its own language. The imaginative curiosity that is always left over feeds into a new book.' Iris Murdoch's 'aesthetic of imperfection', Lorna Sage goes on to say, 'is powerfully attractive because it mocks the critical demand for totalities, and makes fiction seem a living process'.[3]

This being so it seems especially appropriate to be discussing this author while she is still in the process of writing new novels, for each novel, as it appears, is, for all its philosophical searchings and questionings, by no means the 'last word': it merely creates the illusion of finality by virtue of being the most recent. So the act of faith between concludes *The Good Apprentice* (1985) is very moving *because* of its refusal to sum anything up: it leaves the door open for all the different ways in which the characters within the novel and the audience outside the novel choose to read their human experience. Harry and his two sons cross the barriers of mutual misunderstanding for a moment as they drink to what the still suffering Edmund calls vaguely 'good things in the world' aware that they 'might all mean different ones' (p. 522).

The unsettling effect of the endings is bound up with the formal problem of genre, of how to read, as Iris Murdoch tends to move rather disconcertingly between realist and fantasy modes. The question is raised with more than usual acuteness by *The Philosopher's Pupil.* I would like to return briefly to this novel and explore some of the ways in which questions of genre, narrative symbolism and closure are inter-related.

The central symbol in the narrative, the Ennistone Baths, a riotous amalgam of architectural modes, can be seen as an analogy for the structure of the novel as a whole. The novel is a veritable hotch-potch of genres. If we see Tom McCaffrey at its centre it suggests a *bildungsroman* dominated by the quest motif with its corresponding fairy-tale imagery: Tom is in N's archaic language 'pictured somewhat' by Ennistone society 'as setting out on life's journey with a plume in his helmet and a sword at his knee' (p. 118). With George at its centre the genre is detective thriller (Did he attempt to murder his wife? Does he kill John Robert?) Another aspect of the novel, involving various of the characters, George, Alex and possibly Harriet, suggests the Gothic mode, with its ghosts, doubles and subterranean passages conveying horror and psychological impasse. With the Ennistone community as its focus the novel playfully imitates Victorian realism, a mode which is strengthened by N's gossipy coda.

What is the connection between all these plots, all these people? The dominant narrative image of the Baths is curiously bound up with the cause-and-effect structure of the plot. Central to the lengthy description of the Baths is the image of the swimming babies: these recur in some very tender descriptions (pp. 30 and 90). The 'aquatic infants', spontaneous, instinctive, delighting in the water, represent an opposite pole of human existence and experience to that of the philosopher, John Robert, first introduced to us by N as 'tired of his mind' and shown tormented in a hell of endless cerebration. Yet in the plot-structure John Robert and the swimming babies are connected. When the evil-minded George sees the babies, he fantasises about pushing the helpless little bodies under the water but the body he ends up submerging in the Baths is the (already dead?) body of John Robert. As he presses the body under the water his fantasy of drowning the babies slides back into his mind: 'he had the strange feeling that he had performed this ritual before, perhaps many times. He thought, it's just like the dead babies' (p. 536). The connection here is illumined by the larger image of the Ennistone Baths themselves. The spa buildings and relics provide a selective summary of the history of our civilisation, they bear the marks of successive epochs: from the Roman times ('the rudimentary stone image of a goddess, 'perhaps Freya', housed in the Museum) down to our own (the modernisation of the engine-room using the vast resources of present-day technology). As such they suggest Freud's vision of civilisation as founded upon Eros, and rising out of the human need to control Eros; the Baths themselves, partly destroyed and reconstructed through various historical epochs, are similarly raised above and around the generative and regenerative powers of the spa waters.

In this context John Robert Rozanov and the babies suggest opposing and yet connected principles of life. The disillusioned and highly cultured Rozanov represents a pinnacle of our civilisation with its double-edged achievements; the babies 'like funny little animals of some quite other species' (p. 90) are instinctively at home in the fecund waters. And yet John Robert's huge bulk is restored to the spa waters in death. John Robert's death conveys in the novel as a whole a sense of the flux and continuity of human life where distinctions in age and mode of existence are more apparent than real ('Where does one person end and another person begin?' is N's last question). And given the analogy between the spa buildings and human history and between the spa waters and the life-urge or libido, the death of the philosopher suggests the merging of highly civilised and tormented human self-consciousness back into the sea of organic life out of which it has emerged for a relatively brief moment of geological time.

The 'happy endings' for the other characters in the novel appear as a consciously arbitrary tying up of loose ends. So Hattie Meynell after her terrible drama with the philosopher moves into a happy marriage with Tom McCaffrey, a curiously incongruous destiny. Hattie changes her function in the novel several times. We expect to find at first a Jamesian 'blank page', an innocent manipulated young thing caught between American and European cultures, and get instead a disconcertingly intelligent, courageous and even audacious young woman who is strong-willed in her fight for her happiness. She is humanly unpredictable in response to the set assumptions all the others have of her, assumptions which are bound up with conventional notions about femininity and virginity (so that Hattie's femaleness is central to her breaking of patterns). But at the end of the novel Hattie is transformed into a conventional, almost Victorian heroine, led away by a newly assertive Tom, suddenly reaching out for his heart's desire. The novel has abruptly changed mode and in its fairy-tale ending concentrates upon Tom and his quest, at the expense of the much more richly drawn and rather tragic Hattie.

Hattie takes part in both dramas, her grandfather's and Tom's, and has a different function in each. She also has her own brooding inner life which she can share only with Pearl. The author quite deliberately foreshortens Hattie's story in the 'happy ending', reminding the reader, as through the whole device of male narration, of how much human experience *doesn't* get into the novels. This left-overness is suggested earlier by a single curiously proleptic, or anticipatory, phrase which apparently has nothing to do with Hattie's life as we are later shown it: Hattie is described at one point as emerging 'substanceless as a seed into the brown spaces of the landing and the stairs which she was destined to dream about for the rest of her life' (p. 172)—a piece of information to which the elderly N himself couldn't possibly have had access, and which presumably is the direct contribution of the 'certain lady'. The phrase has the effect of extending Hattie's story beyond the framework in which the plot-structure of the novel ironically encloses it.

Because of the interplay of genres, of voices, Hattie remains elusive and a central silence surrounds the most important questions in the novel—the philosopher's moral disintegration, the pupil George's 'convalescence' and the part played in it by his wife, Stella (herself curiously absent, hidden away by N, during the main progress of the novel). The mysterious gaps in the plot also work to subvert set assumptions about erotic love. The erotic experience in *The Philosopher's Pupil* is peculiarly hard to categorise, tending as it does to unfold through the memories of the various characters. Does it take place in fact or in fantasy? Is it heterosexual or homosexual? What is it that binds people together? Certainly in this novel the author has produced some of her most bizarre matchings and mismatchings as she explores the power and vagaries of erotic love.

The kaleidoscopic shifts in the pattern of relationship among Iris Murdoch's characters are a well-known feature of the Murdochian plot. Such pattern-making and breaking can make a social and political point about the relationship of human beings to their community. Iris Murdoch's distinctive presentation of her characters in love is certainly calculated to upset the conventional Western view of society as 'a hierarchy of relationships with the perfect couple at the top'.[4] In consequence it points obliquely to the social and economic pressures which condemn so many people to isolation. In *Bruno's Dream* (1969), for example, Diana's love for the very old, dying Bruno is implicitly contrasted with the worldly entanglement of Will and Adelaide who come together, eventually, with a full eye to social and financial advantages. The 'pointless' love which Diana feels for Bruno at the end is given its full emphasis as a love-relationship by being set in the context of all the other love-relationships which have been explored through-out the novel. Diana, sitting by Bruno's bedside, reflects just before the novel itself ends: 'We've all paired off really, in the end. Miles had got his nurse, Lisa had got Danby. And I've got Bruno. Who would have thought it would work out like that?' (p. 267). Such relationships as that between Diana and Bruno are hard to categorise and do not easily fit into the economical systems (psychological and social) in which we learn to live. Iris Murdoch seems concerned to demonstrate the fragility of such apparently rigid systems. Her concern with what you do with, what happens to, 'left-over' Eros, is related to her playful imitation of male-dominated structures (Whitehall in *The Nice and the Good*, 'theatre-business, management of men' in *The Sea, The Sea*, for example), imitations which are set up to point exactly to the emotional violence which these structures cannot accommodate.

Alasdair MacIntyre, commenting upon the 'inade-quacy of the endings', suggests that the novels may, by virtue of their inconclusiveness, 'quite inadvertently, make a case for the pointlessness of morality, not, as our modern Neoplatonists intend, in the sense of a high-minded disclaiming of any this-worldly *telos,* any form of social life as the good life for man, but in a way which makes morality appear to be in the end no more than an aesthetically engaging and compelling phenomenon'.[5] I have been arguing here that pattern-breaking in Iris Murdoch's novels *can* have social as well as aesthetic significance. The world as Iris Murdoch shows it is decentred, full of displaced persons, a world where the old stable social and ethical systems no longer provide security. In her relentless probing of the less acceptable areas of the psyche, of the various ways in which we lay waste our creative energies, and of the power struggles which make up life in an aggressive society, Iris Murdoch offers a surprisingly fresh and radical vision of the human (and, as I have argued, in many ways, specifically female) struggle both for self-definition and for connection with others. It is in these areas that Iris Murdoch reveals an in-touchness with some vital feminist issues, and can speak to the feminist need for re-readings of the world, even though she cannot ultimately be claimed as a feminist writer.

There remains an undeniable split in Iris Murdoch's writing, a split between cerebration and emotion, mind and body, philosophy and poetry, 'masculine' and 'feminine' spheres of experience and attainment (John Robert Rozanov and the babies in the swimming pool?). It reflects faithfully enough the divisions in our traditional Western culture, the culture of which Iris Murdoch's novels are so rich and remarkable a storehouse. But in focusing upon and exploring these dualities as she does, Iris Murdoch is able to turn the divided self to creative account, making Irigarayan play with the unvoiced possibilities in the dominant discourse. The inconsistencies which appear at the various levels of style, characterisation and genre work as a creative unsettling of various reader-expectations.

In a review of *The Good Apprentice*[6] Stephen Medcalf notes how in Iris Murdoch's hands 'parable' has a way of turning into 'experiment': (Edward's search for his natural father, Jesse, finds a parallel in the Biblical story of the Prodigal Son):

> *The Good Apprentice* begins with an explicit reference to Edward as the prodigal son, and his crime, return to his father, and redemption follow the parable exactly enough. But for Miss Murdoch a novel is a means of testing reality. It is not surprising that in her world, where authority is always suspect, the father of Christ's parable becomes fallible and an enchanter, and is only in Edward's awareness the means of his recovery.

This last statement beautifully conveys the paradoxical nature of Iris Murdoch's relationship to the centre (authority; certainty; truth; God). She at once intensely questions it (and with it the 'centrality' of so many of our masculine assumptions) and at the same time recognises the deep human need to be continually re-seeking and re-defining the centre. It is a paradox which will speak to those women readers who are attempting to recognise and move beyond the personal and cultural myths which have shaped their individual beings. Through such mapping out we can all seek to discover our own relationship to the centre: 'The whole matrix shifts and we shift with it', reflects Anne Cavidge in *Nuns and Soldiers*, as she gives up for the moment her own quest for certainty. Accordingly, Iris Murdoch's work with its delighted search for imperfection, its prolific creativity and its refusal to rest content with conclusions has much to show its women readers as, in Julia Kristeva's phrase, 'subjects-in-the-making, subjects-on-trial'.[7] And in the end it bears eloquent testimony to the human capacity—circumscribed but nevertheless inspiriting—for change and renewal.

Notes

Chapter 1: Introduction: Questing Heroes

1. Elaine Showalter, 'Feminist Criticism in the Wilderness', in *Critical Inquiry*, 8 (1981), 179–206; repr. in Elizabeth Abel (ed.), *Writing and Sexual Difference*, pp. 9–36; p. 30.
2. See, for example, Richard Todd, *Iris Murdoch* (London and New York: Methuen, 1984), p. 74: 'it does seem to be the case that the first-person narration suits not just Murdoch's technical gifts but the presentation of her
5. theme in novel form'.
3. Elizabeth Dipple, *Iris Murdoch: Work for the Spirit* (London: Methuen, 1982), p. 88.
4. Iris Murdoch 'On "God" and "Good" ', in *The Sovereignty of Good* (London and Henley: Routledge & Kegan Paul, 1970), p. 53.
5. Iris Murdoch, *The Fire and the Sun: Why Plato Banished the Artists* (Oxford: Oxford University Press, 1977, reprinted 1978), p. 80.
6. Patrick Parrinder, 'Pilgrim's Progress: The Novels of B.S. Johnson (1933–73)', *Critical Quarterly*, vol. 19, no. 2, 45–59; p. 47.

7. Iris Murdoch, *Sartre: Romantic Rationalist* (1953; London: Fontana/Collins, 1967), p. 59.
8. 'The true *logos* falls silent in the presence of the highest (ineffable) truth, but the art object cherishes its volubility, it cherishes itself not the truth and wishes to be indestructible and eternal.' Iris Murdoch, *The Fire and the Sun*, pp. 65–6.
9. In Lacanian terminology the symbolic order is the order instituted within the individual human being by language. The child enters this order when it comes to language. Lacan contrasts the symbolic order, whose carrier is the father figure, with the imaginary order—the sensory 'given' of experience, the order of perception and hallucination.
10. Mary Jacobus, 'The Question' of Language: Men of Maxims and *The Mill on the Floss*' in *Critical Inquiry*, 8 (1981), 207–22; repr. in *Writing and Sexual Difference*, ed. Elizabeth Abel (Brighton: Harvester, 1982), pp. 37–52.
11. Mary Jacobus, 'The Question of Language', p. 37.
12. *ibid.*, p. 38.
13. *ibid.*, p. 40.
14. *ibid.*, pp. 38–9.
15. Annis V. Pratt, 'The New Feminist Criticisms: Exploring the History of the New Space', in *Beyond Intellectual Sexism: A New Woman, A New Reality*, ed. Joan I. Roberts (New York: David McKay, 1976), p. 183.
16. Sandra Gilbert and Susan Gubar, *The Madwoman in the Attic: The Woman Writer and the Nineteenth-Century Literary Imagination*, (New Haven and London: Yale University Press, 1979), p. 70. For the relevant context see the whole of the chapter 'Infection in the Sentence: The Woman Writer and the Anxiety of Authorship', pp. 45–92.
17. Roland Barthes, *The Pleasure of the Text*, trans. Richard Miller (New York: Hill and Wang, 1975), p. 10. Quoted in Teresa de Lauretis, *Alice doesn't: Feminism, Semiotics, Cinema* (London and Basingstoke: Macmillan, 1984), pp. 107–8.
18. Teresa de Lauretis, *Alice doesn't*, Chapter 5, 'Desire in Narrative', pp. 103–57.
19. *ibid.*, pp. 124–5.
20. Peter J. Conradi, *Iris Murdoch: The Saint and the Artist* (London and Basingstoke: Macmillan, 1986), pp. 83–4.

21. *ibid.*, p. 84.
22. *ibid.*, p. 83.
23. Teresa de Lauretis, *Alice doesn't*, p. 12.
24. A.S. Byatt, *Degrees of Freedom: The Novels of Iris Murdoch* (London: Chatto and Windus, 1965), p. 204.

Chapter 2: The Role of the Narrator

1. A.S. Byatt, *Iris Murdoch* (London: Longman, 1976), p. 19.
2. Douglas Jefferson, 'Iris Murdoch: the Novelist and the Moralist' in *The Uses of Fiction: Essays on the Modern Novel in Honour of Arnold Kettle*, ed. Douglas Jefferson and Graham Martin (Milton Keynes: Open University Press, 1982), p. 263.
3. Elizabeth Dipple, *Iris Murdoch: Work for the Spirit*, p. 152.
4. *ibid.*, p. 152.
5. Freud in *The Interpretation of Dreams* describes the ways in which dreams 'reproduce *logical connection* by *simultaneity in time*'. His observation on dreams, 'Whenever they give us two elements close together, this guarantees that there is some specially intimate connection between what corresponds to them among the dream-thoughts', seems to me to offer a vital clue to the structure of *The Italian Girl*. See *The Standard Edition of the Complete Psychological Works of Sigmund Freud*, ed. James Strachey (London: Hogarth Press and the Institute of Psycho-analysis, 1953–74), vol. IV, pp. 314–5.
6. Quoted above; Chapter One, p. 11.
7. Freud, *Complete Psychological Works*, vol. XVI, p. 376.
8. The painting is a recurrent motif in Iris Murdoch's novels; she discussed her personal responses to it more particularly in a programme made by Border Television as part of a series, *Revelations*, for Channel Four Television and broadcast on 22 September 1984.
9. Joyce Carol Oates, review of *The Philosopher's Pupil* in the *New York Times*, 17 July 1983.
10. Tilly Olsen, *Silences* (London: Virago, 1980), p. 249.

Chapter 3: Degrees of Confinement: The Plots and the Settings

1. Elizabeth Dipple, *Iris Murdoch: Work for the Spirit*, p. 82.
2. A.S. Byatt, *Degrees of Freedom*, p. 213.
3. Robert Taubman, review of *The Philosopher's Pupil* in *The London Review of Books*, 19 May–2 June 1983.
4. I am indebted for the general thought here to Lucy Goodison, 'Really Being in Love Means Wanting to Live in a Different World', in *Sex and Love: New Thoughts on Old Contradictions*, ed. Sue Cartledge and Joanna Ryan (London: The Women's Press, 1983), p. 56.
5. Notably Iris Murdoch's own essay, 'The Sovereignty of Good Over Other Concepts', in *The Sovereignty of Good*; see especially p. 99 and pp. 103–4.
6. Lorna Sage, 'The Pursuit of Imperfection', *Critical Quarterly*, vol. 19, no. 2 (1977), 61–8.
7. I follow Richard Todd's suggestion in *Iris Murdoch*, p. 73.
8. Judith Wilt, *Ghosts of the Gothic: Austen, Eliot and Lawrence* (Princeton, N.J.: Princeton University Press, 1980), p. 31. The context (pp. 31–41), an account of Ann Radcliffe's *The Italian* (1797), is of fascinating relevance to *The Time of the Angels*.
9. Iris Murdoch uses the phrase 'switch [or shift] of *gestalt*' several times in her novels. (The *gestalt* in perceptual psychology denotes the particular perception of a foreground/background configuration.) The phrase is tellingly used in *The Black Prince*, where Bradley's first erring perception of Julian as a young boy, chanting and scattering flower petals, gives way to the realisation (achieved through two distinct 'switches of *gestalt*') that Julian is a girl who is throwing away the fragments of torn paper, love-letters (pp. 55–6). As is characteristic of Iris Murdoch the visual realisation carries with it the sense of an emotional and moral switch of *gestalt*, the violent change of perspective which often accompanies the experience of 'falling in love'.

Chapter 4: The Sibyl's Cave: Narrative Symbol

1. Iris Murdoch, review of Elias Canetti's *Crowds and Power*, in *The Spectator*, 7 September 1962, quoted by A.S. Byatt, *Iris Murdoch*, p. 29.
2. See, for instance, her comments on 'myth' in Frank Kermode, 'The House of Fiction: Interviews with Seven English Novelists', *Partisan Review*, vol. 30, no. 1, Spring 1963, 61–82; repr. in *The Novel Today*, ed. Malcolm Bradbury (London: Fontana/Collins, 1977), pp. 111–35.
3. Elaine Showalter, 'Feminist Criticism in the Wilderness' in Elizabeth Abel, *Writing and Sexual Difference*, p. 34. The last sentence is quoted by Showalter from her own 'Literary Criticism', *Signs* 1 (Winter, 1975), 435–60; p. 435.
4. A.S. Byatt, *Iris Murdoch*, p. 34. See also Byatt's argument in *Degrees of Freedom*, pp. 75–9.
5. A.S. Byatt, *Degrees of Freedom*, p. 197.
6. Iris Murdoch, speaking on *Revelations* (Border Television/ Channel Four), 22 September 1984.
7. Elaine Showalter, 'Feminist Criticism in the Wilderness' in Elizabeth Abel, *Writing and Sexual Difference*, p. 34.
8. Alasdair MacIntyre, review of *Iris Murdoch: Work for the Spirit* by Elizabeth Dipple, in *The London Review of Books*, vol. 4, no. 10, pp. 15–16.
9. Adrienne Rich, 'Living in the Cave', *Adrienne Rich's Poetry*, ed. Barbara Charlesworth Gelpi and Albert Gelpi (New York: Norton, 1975), p. 72; quoted in Gilbert and Gubar, *The Madwoman in the Attic*, p. 102.
10. Gilbert and Gubar, *The Madwoman in the Attic*, p. 93.
11. *ibid.*, p. 95.
12. Luce Irigaray, *Speculum, de l'autre femme*, 'L'$\mu\sigma\tau\acute{e}\beta\alpha$ de Platon' (Minuit: Paris, 1974).
13. *ibid.*, p. 306: 'Oppositions qui supposent toujours le *saut* d'un pire à un mieux. Une ascension, un déplacement(?) vers le haut, une progression le long d'une ligne. Verticale. Phallique?' (my translation).
14. Iris Murdoch, interview with John Haffenden, *Literary Review*, 58, April 1983, 31–5.
15. Charles may be compared with a very different kind of hermit, Father Bernard, who retires to a Greek chapel at

the end of *The Philosopher's Pupil* and writes to N: 'It is vitally *important* that I live now in a *cave*. Well, it is a tiny abandoned chapel, a slit made in a rock' (p. 552). From here he preaches a 'charmless holiness' and arrives at a pared-down understanding of his religious faith, 'The inner is the outer, the outer is the inner: an old story, but who really understands it?' (p. 552).

16. For an account of the classical Sibyl's Cave and its associations with rites of spiritual initiation in the Cretan mysteries see W.F. Jackson Knight, *Cumaean Gates: A Reference of the Sixth Aeneid to the Initiation Pattern* (Oxford, 1936), *passim*.

17. See, for example, Luce Irigaray's 'When Our Lips Speak Together' (trans. Carolyn Burke, *Signs*, vol. 6, no. 1, Autumn, 1980, 66–79): 'Light is not violent or deadly for us. The sun does not rise or set simply. Night and day are mingled in our gazes, our gestures, our bodies. Strictly speaking, we cast no shadow. There is no chance that one might become the darker double of the other' (p. 78).

18. *The Fire and the Sun*, pp. 88–9.

19. Richard Todd, *Iris Murdoch*, p. 94.

20. *The Fire and the Sun*, p. 86.

21. ibid., p. 87.

22. It is interesting, by the way, that Iris Murdoch is so aware of the 'masculine' assumptions and images embedded in Platonic discourse, although she reproduces these without evident criticism in her essay: 'Plato often uses images of paternity. Art launches philosophy as it launches religion, and it was necessary for Plato, as it was for the evangelists, to write if the Word was not to be sterile and the issue of the Father was to be recognized as legitimate' (*The Fire and the Sun*, p. 88).

23. Walter Allen, *Tradition and Dream: The English and American Novel from the Twenties to Our Time* (London: Phoenix House, 1964), p. 284.

Chapter 5: Making an Exit: Closures and Conclusions

1. Elizabeth Dipple, *Iris Murdoch: Work for the Spirit*, p. 157.
2. *ibid.*, p. 85.
3. Lorna Sage, 'The Pursuit of Imperfection', pp. 67–8.
4. I quote here from Lucy Goodison, 'Really Being in Love Means Wanting to Live in a Different World', in Sue Cartledge and Joanna Ryan, *Sex and Love*, p. 65.
5. *The London Review of Books*, vol. 4, no. 10, pp. 15–16 (review cited in Chapter 5, n.8).
6. *The Times Literary Supplement*, 27 September 1985.
7. Julia Kristeva, extract from 'Oscillation du "pouvoir" au "refus"' (*Tel quel*, Summer 1974); trans. Marilyn A. August in *New French Feminisms: An Anthology*, ed. Elaine Marks and Isabelle de Courtivron (Amherst: University of Massachusetts Press, 1980; Brighton: Harvester, 1981), p. 167.

Select Bibliography

Works consulted in connection with this study

Major works by Iris Murdoch

Novels (the dates refer to the first editions, published by Chatto and Windus, London).

Under the Net, 1954.
The Flight from the Enchanter, 1955.
The Sandcastle, 1957.
The Bell, 1958.
A Severed Head, 1961.
An Unofficial Rose, 1962.
The Unicorn, 1963.
The Italian Girl, 1964.
The Red and the Green, 1965.
The Time of the Angels, 1966.
The Nice and the Good, 1968.
Bruno's Dream, 1969.

Select Bibliography

A Fairly Honourable Defeat, 1970.
An Accidental Man, 1971.
The Black Prince, 1973.
The Sacred and Profane Love Machine, 1974.
A Word Child, 1975.
Henry and Cato, 1976.
The Sea, The Sea, 1978.
Nuns and Soldiers, 1980.
The Philosopher's Pupil, 1983.
The Good Apprentice, 1985.

Plays

A Severed Head (with J.B. Priestley) (London: Chatto & Windus, 1964).
The Italian Girl (with James Saunders) (London and New York: Samuel French, 1968).
The Three Arrows and *The Servants and the Snow* (London: Chatto & Windus, 1973).

Poetry

A Year of Birds (with engravings by Reynolds Stone) (Tisbury, Wilts: Compton Press, 1978).

Books on Philosophy

Sartre: Romantic Rationalist (Cambridge: Bowes & Bowes, 1953; London: Fontana/Collins, 1967; second edition, Brighton: Harvester, 1980).
The Sovereignty of Good (London: Routledge & Kegan Paul, 1970)
The Fire and the Sun: Why Plato Banished the Artists (Oxford: Oxford University Press, 1977).

Essays (a selection)

'The Novelist as Metaphysician', *The Listener*, 16 March 1950, 473–6.

'Nostalgia for the Particular', *Proceedings of the Artistotelian Society*, 52 (1952), 243–60.
'T.S. Eliot as a Moralist', in *T.S. Eliot: A Symposium for his Seventieth Birthday*, ed. Neville Braybrooke (London: Rupert Hart-Davis, 1958).
'The Sublime and the Good', *Chicago Review*, 13 (Autumn 1959), 42–55.
'The Sublime and the Beautiful Revisited', *Yale Review*, 49 (1959), 247–71.
'Against Dryness: A Polemical Sketch' *Encounter*, 16 (January 1961), 16–20; repr. in *The Novel Today*, ed. Malcolm Bradbury (London: Fontana/Collins, 1977), pp. 23–31.
'Mass, Might and Myth', review of *Crowds and Power* by Elias Canetti, *Spectator*, 7 September 1962, 337–8.
'The Darkness of Practical Reason', *Encounter*, 27 July 1966, 46–50.
'Existentialists and Mystics' in *Essays and Poems Presented to Lord David Cecil*, ed. W.W. Robson (London: Constable, 1970), pp. 169–83.

Interviews (a selection)

Michael O. Bellamy, 'An Interview with Iris Murdoch', *Wisconsin Studies in Contemporary Literature* 18 (1977), 129–40.
John Haffenden, 'In Conversation with Iris Murdoch', *Literary Review*, 58 (April 1983), 31–5.
Frank Kermode, 'The House of Fiction: Interviews with Seven English Novelists', *Partisan Review*, vol. 30, no. 1 (1963), 61–82; repr. in *The Novel Today*, ed. Malcolm Bradbury (London: Fontana/Collins, 1977).
Bryan Magee, 'Philosophy and Literature' in *Men of Ideas: Some Creators of Contemporary Philosophy* (London: BBC Publications, 1978), pp. 262–84.
W.K. Rose, 'Iris Murdoch, informally', *London Magazine* (new series) 8 (June 1968), 59–73.

Critical Works on Iris Murdoch

Books

Byatt, A.S., *Degrees of Freedom: The Novels of Iris Murdoch* (London: Chatto and Windus, 1965).
——, *Iris Murdoch* (London: Longman, 1976).
Chevalier, Jean-Louis (ed.), *Rencontres avec Iris Murdoch* (Caen, France: Centre de Recherches de Littérature et Linguistique des Pays de Langue Anglaise, 1978).
Conradi, Peter J., *Iris Murdoch: The Saint and the Artist* (London and Basingstoke: Macmillan, 1986).
Dipple, Elizabeth, *Iris Murdoch: Work for the Spirit* (London: Methuen, 1982).
Todd, Richard, *Iris Murdoch: The Shakespearian Interest,* (London: Vision, 1979).
——, *Iris Murdoch* (London and New York: Methuen, 1984).
Wolfe, Peter, *The Disciplined Heart: Iris Murdoch and her Novels* (Columbia: University of Missouri Press, 1966).

Essays and Articles

Bradbury, Malcolm, ' "A House Fit for Free Characters": Iris Murdoch and *Under the Net'* in *Possibilites: Essays on the State of the Novel* (London: Oxford University Press, 1973), pp. 231–46.
Conradi, Peter J., 'The Metaphysical Hostess: the Cult of Personal Relations in the Modern English Novel', *ELH,* 48 (1981), 427–53.
Jefferson, Douglas, 'Iris Murdoch: the Novelist and the Moralist' in *The Uses of Fiction: Essays on the Modern Novel in Honour of Arnold Kettle,* ed. Douglas Jefferson and Graham Martin (Milton Keynes: Open University Press, 1982).
Sage, Lorna, 'The Pursuit of Imperfection', *Critical Quarterly,* vol. 19, no. 2 (1977), 61–8.

Critical Theory and Background

Abel, Elizabeth (ed.), *Writing and Sexual Difference* (Brighton: Harvester, 1982).

Beauvoir, Simone de, *The Second Sex*, trans. H.M. Parshley (Harmondsworth: Penguin, 1972).

Cixous, Hélène, 'Le rire de la méduse', *L'Arc*, 61 (1975), 3–54; trans. Keith Cohen and Paula Cohen, 'The Laugh of the Medusa', *Signs*, 1 (1976) 875–93; repr. *New French Feminisms: An Anthology*, ed. Elaine Marks and Isabelle de Courtivron (q.v.), pp. 245–64.

Cartledge, Sue and Ryan, Joanna (eds.), *Sex and Love: New Thoughts on Old Contradictions* (London: The Women's Press, 1983).

Culler, Jonathan, *On Deconstruction: Theory and Criticism after Structuralism* (Ithaca: Cornell University Press, 1982; London: Routledge & Kegan Paul, 1983).

Fetterly, Judith, *The Resisting Reader: A Feminist Approach to American Fiction* (Bloomington: Indiana University Press, 1978).

Freud, Sigmund, *The Standard Edition of the Complete Psychological Works of Sigmund Freud*, ed. James Strachey (London: Hogarth Press and the Institute of Psychoanalysis, 1953–74), 24 vols.

Gilbert, Sandra and Gubar, Susan, *The Madwoman in the Attic: The Woman Writer and the Nineteenth-Century Literary Imagination* (New Haven and London: Yale University Press, 1979).

Irigaray, Luce, *Ce sexe qui n'en est pas un* (Paris: Minuit, 1977).

——, 'When Our Lips Speak Together' (*Ce sexe qui n'en est pas un*), trans. Carolyn Burke, *Signs*, vol. 6, no. 1 (Autumn 1980), 66–79.

——, *Speculum, de l'autre femme* 'L'ὑστέβα de Platon', (Paris: Minuit, 1974).

Jacobus, Mary, 'The Question of Language: Men of Maxims and *The Mill on the Floss*' in *Critical Inquiry*, 8 (1981), 207–22; repr. in Elizabeth Abel (ed.), *Writing and Sexual Difference* (q.v.), pp. 37–52.

——, *Women Writing and Writing About Women* (London: Croom Helm, 1979).

Kristeva, Julia, *Desire in Language* (New York: Columbia University Press, 1980).

——, 'La femme, ce n'est jamais ça' *Tel quel*, 59 (1974), 19–24.

Lacan, Jacques, *Ecrits: A Selection*, trans. Alan Sheridan (London: Tavistock, 1977).

de Lauretis, Teresa, *Alice doesn't: Feminism, Semiotics, Cinema* (London and Basingstoke: Macmillan, 1984).

Marks, Elaine, and Courtivron, Isabelle de (eds.), *New French Feminisms: An Anthology* (Amherst: University of Massachussetts Press, 1980; Brighton: Harvester, 1981).

Olsen, Tilly, *Silences* (London: Virago, 1980).

Roberts, Joan I. (ed.), *Beyond Intellectual Sexism: A New Woman, A New Reality* (New York: David McKay, 1976).

Showalter, Elaine, 'Literary Criticism', *Signs* 1 (Winter (1975), 435–60.

——, 'Feminist Criticism in the Wilderness', *Critical Inquiry*, 8 (1981), 179–206; repr. in Elizabeth Abel (ed.), *Writing and Sexual Difference* (q.v.), pp. 9–36.

Wilt, Judith, *Ghosts of the Gothic: Austen, Eliot and Lawrence* (Princeton, N.J.: Princeton University Press, 1980).

Index

Index